# The Sound of Murder

BY THE SAME AUTHOR

They Almost Escaped
No Hiding Place

PERCY HOSKINS

# The Sound of Murder

 JOHN LONG, LONDON

JOHN LONG LIMITED
*3 Fitzroy Square, London W1*

AN IMPRINT OF THE HUTCHINSON GROUP

London Melbourne Sydney Auckland
Wellington Johannesburg Cape Town
and agencies throughout the world

*First published 1973*

*This book has been set in Times type, printed in Great Britain
on antique wove paper by Anchor Press, and
bound by Wm. Brendon, both of Tiptree, Essex*
ISBN 0 09 115680 7

# Contents

# Acknowledgments

I am indebted to the author and publishers of *Murder was my Business* by John du Rose (W. H. Allen) and to the editor of the *Medico-Legal Journal* for permission to reproduce material in this book. I am also grateful to Beaverbrook Newspapers for supplying nearly all the pictures.

# Illustrations

Detective Chief Superintendent John du Rose at 'nude murders' H.Q.

The author with James Callaghan and Sir Ronald Howe (*Press Association*)

'For murder, though it may no tongue, will speak
With most miraculous organ.'

*Hamlet*: II, ii

# Author's Note

I was born on Holy Innocent's Day, in 1904, in Bridport, the small Dorset town where they used to make the hangman's rope. So perhaps, in a way, I was destined for a career as a recorder of human frailties.

It is a career that now spans almost half a century, and the frailties have been many, and varied. I have known blackmailers, arsonists, spies, sexual deviates, drug peddlers, thieves, swindlers, confidence tricksters and many, many murderers.

Of all the frailties, the worst is murder. There is no end to its variety.

In the days when, rightly in my opinion, it was punishable by death—by the hangman's rope, the 'Bridport Dagger' as the Elizabethan poets called it—there was an awful fascination in recording the uncovering of murder and the pursuit of the criminal responsible.

In this book I have selected some of the murder cases, and some of the famous Murder Squad investigators, that have come my way in a career that began before most of today's policemen were born.

There is one linking theme. That unique, intangible quality: the sound of murder.

P.H.

# 1   The Lady Vanishes

Everything you experience for the first time in life holds a special place in the mind. Take my word for it, nothing measures up to the shock inflicted by your first acquaintance with murder.

The Thorne case was my first as a crime reporter. I interviewed the man later convicted of murder before he was questioned by Scotland Yard. I even guessed—correctly—where he had hidden the body of his victim. I sat through his trial in March, 1925, and saw a judge don the black cap for the first time, a moment never to be forgotten by any man.

But these are not the only reasons why I remember this case so well. Today, nearly fifty years and many hundreds of murder stories later, I still have a lingering, uneasy doubt in my own mind whether this man Thorne should have been hanged. I invite you to be his second jury: though if your verdict should differ from the first, you cannot help him now.

Norman Thorne, aged twenty-four, was a chicken farmer at a village called Blackness, near Crowborough, in Sussex. He was a man of completely respectable background, as far as anyone knew. He was a Sunday school teacher and boys' club organiser. He was stockily built, with a pleasant enough face and a shock of wild black hair.

Thorne was like a lot of other young men who found it hard to settle down after the 1914–18 war (he served in the Army, towards the end). He took first one job, then another.

Finally, in 1922, with help from his father, Norman Thorne made a start raising chickens on that desolate, muddy patch at Blackness.

One year earlier he had met a girl in London, perhaps as lonely and unsettled as he was. Her name was Elsie Cameron. She was—in looks and personality, anyway—no great catch: pale and plain, with short-bobbed hair and spectacles to aid pronounced short sight. She fell violently in love with him. In turn she became girlfriend, mistress and then fiancée.

To save money, Thorne quit his digs in Crowborough and furnished one of the plain wooden brood houses on his farm. He hung a few pictures on the walls and put a desk at the far end. It was heated by a stove whose hot coals lit up the dingy hut with a faint glow after the oil lamps had been turned out. A steel-framed bed made a daytime settee. There was just room underneath for Thorne to jam the chickens' feed buckets.

Many a night Elsie travelled down, and spent it on the farm with Thorne. One day, towards the last week of November 1924, she wrote to her fiancée:

'I feel sick every day, and things will soon be noticeable to everybody, and I want to be married before Christmas . . . and it will be obvious to everyone soon after that. Also, you must let your people know as soon as you can.'

Elsie believed herself to be pregnant.

There was one complication. Since moving to Crowborough to run his chicken farm, Norman Thorne had met a local belle called Elizabeth Coldicott, and had fallen head over heels in love with *her*.

Miss Coldicott, of course, was in no way connected with the events that followed, nor was she called as a witness at the trial. She was just a pretty girl who had happened to meet Thorne. But, by her very existence, she was to provide the prosecution with an age-old motive for murder.

For some time Elsie had been putting pressure on Norman Thorne to marry her. He told her he had met someone else,

Maybe this was why Elsie told him she was pregnant, to try
to force him into marriage. Medical evidence showed later
that she was not, in fact, expecting a child. But whether she
genuinely believed this to be so at the time, or she had lied to
influence Thorne, we shall never know.

On 5 December, a cold and overcast day, Elsie said goodbye
to her parents in Willesden, North West London, and set out
for Crowborough. She was determined not to come back without a wedding ring.

She never came back at all.

Crowborough is only forty miles from London. During that
short journey, or so it seemed to her parents at the time, Elsie
simply vanished without trace. After a week of silence, her
father sent Thorne a telegram asking what had happened.

Thorne wired, then wrote—a rambling and confused letter
—to say one thing: that she had never arrived at his farm. 'I
cannot say any more,' he finished his letter, 'as needless to
say I am worried and upset.'

Elsie's father at once contacted the local police. They made
certain inquiries. There was no direct evidence of murder, but
quite clearly something untoward had happened to the missing
Miss Cameron. They in turn called in Scotland Yard.

When the Yard investigation opened, in January 1925, I
was sitting in the old *Evening Standard* office in Fleet Street
writing (by hand) my column as a young, West End showbiz
reporter.

We had no such luxuries in those days as a Scotland Yard
press bureau, manned by three dozen civil servants, to dole
out news to reporters telephoning from their offices. Every
scrap of information that came your way then was gleaned by
personal contact.

'Hoskins,' said the news editor of the day. 'I need someone to
go to Crowborough. There's a girl missing and the Yard have
been called in. You're the only man available. On your way.'

So, with many doubts and misgivings, I quit show business
and started my career as crime reporter. By a lucky break,

Chief Detective Inspector John Gillan, the Yard man in charge of the investigation, was on the same train to Crowborough. His sergeant was the son of a superintendent from my home town at Bridport, and knew me by sight.

'Come on,' he said, 'and I'll introduce you to the Guv'nor.'

Gillan was a brisk, confident man, with piercing dark eyes. We spoke about Thorne, at that moment only a name to both of us.

'Why don't *you* go and call on him?' said Gillan. 'See what he has to say. Weigh him up. Let me know your reactions.'

A good detective—and the Yard has had many over the years—will listen to information and ideas from any and every source, then sift them all to see what, if anything, he can use. It is part and parcel of his job.

Thorne received me courteously enough. He told me, as he had already told Elsie's parents, that his fiancée had never reached the farm in December and that he had no idea where she was. His Leghorn chickens squawked and clacked around our feet as we walked in the mud. Thorne spoke of his 'terrible' anxiety about Elsie. He swore he would help in every way to find her.

At that moment, the village postman knocked and delivered two letters. Thorne read through them as we walked back down the path. Without a word he handed them to me. They needed no explanation. Reduced to three words in each case was all the gossip and rumour that bubbled and boiled in every house in the village.

'YOU . . . MURDERER!'

'Look what they're saying about me!' cried Thorne. 'How can I stop them and their gossip?'

'That's easy,' I told him. 'And there's only one way to do it. You've got to invite the police to come in and dig up every inch of your farm.'

Thorne hesitated. Then he said: 'That's an idea. I'll do it.' Pause. 'I don't mind what the police do, *as long as they don't disturb my chickens.*'

We shook hands and said goodbye. Later that evening, over a glass of whisky at the hotel, Gillan asked me how I had got on. I told him, mentioned the postman's call with his poison pen letters, and Thorne's reaction to my suggestion about digging up the farm.

I said: 'And that's where I reckon the body is—under the chicken run.'

Gillan already had a house to house inquiry going on, seeking some clue to the whereabouts of the missing woman. Whatever he thought privately, he needed something a lot more positive than a reporter's guess before he could apply for a search warrant. Within hours, he had it.

A local woman who had just returned from Christmas holiday said she had seen Elsie turning in to the farm entrance on 5 December, the day she had left home at Willesden. At once Gillan sent a message to Thorne, asking him to call in at the local police station. A sergeant brought him in. Gillan told his men to start digging.

While Thorne sat there, fretting, waiting and wondering, Gillan decided to start the questioning with a daring piece of bluff. He sent out for a pair of spectacles exactly like those Elsie Cameron had worn when she called at the farm. He dropped them in soft mud, so the rims and frames and eye-pieces were coated. He took off his own shoes and put on a muddy pair of Wellington boots. Then he marched back into the interview room and, without a word, threw the glasses on the table in front of Thorne.

There was a long silence. Finally Thorne raised his head, looked away from the spectacles and straight at Gillan.

'So you have found her,' he said.

He had fallen into Gillan's trap. So far, police at the farm had only unearthed a suitcase. Next day, after driving the chickens from their run, they found what was left of Elsie Cameron. She had been dismembered. Legs and trunk, wrapped in sacking, and her head, rammed into a tin box, were found under the run where he and I had stood talking.

Thorne, caught up in a web of lies, was charged with her murder. Tho police case against him looked overwhelming. It still does.

Why, then, does this faint but nagging doubt of mine persist after so many years? The answer lies in the trial at Lewes Assize.

Apart from the drama and heightened tension surrounding every trial for murder in those days of capital punishment, this case also set the stage for the first of many courtroom duels between two of the country's top pathologists.

It was *their* findings, even more than that of the detectives involved, that were to decide the ultimate fate of Norman Thorne, whether he would hang by the neck until he was dead or walk out of the building scot free. And that is what worries me.

Sir Bernard Spilsbury, that eminent, calm and totally convincing Home Office expert, appeared for the Crown. Few medical witnesses have enjoyed a greater reputation than Spilsbury's, at that time. Laymen regarded him as well nigh infallible.

Dr. Robert Bronte, a fiery and passionate Irishman, appeared for the defence.

Their qualified opinions, their expert conclusions, drawn from separate and equally painstaking examination, were directly opposed. One was clearly wrong, but which one? A life depended on it.

Thorne's story, so different from the lies he first told me, was now this. He now admitted Elsie had reached the farm. He told how they had tea together in his hut on 5 December, and how they quarrelled over the other girl. He said Elsie wanted to stay the night. He tried, without success, to persuade a neighbour to put her up. She told him she was expecting a baby.

Thorne insisted he left her in the hut while he went out to meet Miss Coldicott. He had to do this, he explained, because she had been shopping and he was needed to carry the heavy bags. Then, when he got back to the hut around eleven-thirty that night, he found Elsie dead. She had hanged herself by his clothes line. He went in to find her body dangling from the crossbeam. With that, said Thorne, he panicked.

He did not go to the police because he felt no-one would believe she had killed herself. He cut the rope, the body fell to the floor. He knelt and stripped it and burned the clothing.

'Then,' he said, 'I got a hacksaw, and sawed off her legs and head by the glow of the fire.'

Sometime towards the end of that dreadful night, he buried what had once been Elsie Cameron beneath the chicken run.

This was the vital issue the two pathologists had to help the jury decide. Was Thorne telling the truth at last? Was she dead when he came home, did he panic and dismember the body before burial? Or did he, as the Crown maintained, kill her with blows from a cudgel—maybe before he went out to meet her rival, Elizabeth—and cold-bloodedly saw the body up on his return before trying to hide it?

Spilsbury was adamant. He insisted death was due to shock and that multiple bruises found on the body were caused *before* death. He said two heavy blows on the head were inflicted last of all: one of them, to the temple, was very severe. An Indian club found at the farm might have been the murder weapon.

Sir Bernard also said that marks found on Elsie's neck— marks with which the defence made great play—were caused not by a rope, but by the natural creases of age.

'I found nothing,' he declared 'externally or internally to justify the proposition that there had been attempted hanging.

'Death was caused by shock due to bruises on the face, head, legs and feet, to the combined effect of all the bruises. I found nothing else to account for death.'

Dr. Bronte challenged every word of Spilsbury's findings. He swore the grooves found on the girl's neck were consistent with hanging. And he was backed by no fewer than nine doctors, six of whom were actually prepared to say the great Spilsbury was *wrong* in his findings. Bronte maintained the

B

bruising was caused when the body was cut down and crashed to the floor of the hut.

The little Irishman was a dramatic witness. He even stood in the witness box and slipped a noose round his own neck, in an effort to prove that the absence of some marks could have been caused by the girl's hair coming between neck and rope.

Sir Henry Curtis-Bennett, famous counsel who led for the Crown, reminded the jury that according to Thorne's own evidence this could not be so. He had testified that Elsie's hair was outside the noose when he cut her down.

It was virtually all over.

After an absence of only twenty minutes, the jury filed back. Their verdict: guilty. The appeal failed. On a bright spring day in April 1925, chicken farmer Norman Thorne was duly hanged at Wandsworth Jail.

There has been a lot of comment, since the day of the trial, on this point of Spilsbury's 'infallibility'. Did his reputation finally tip the scales unfairly?

That Thorne lied from the outset is unarguable. That he was playing a double game with fiancée and girl friend is unarguable. That he dismembered and hid the body was fully admitted. That his conduct, from beginning to end, was sure to forfeit all sympathy from the jury—any jury—is accepted.

And yet; and yet.

One of those two pathologists had to be totally wrong, and why might it not have been, just for once, the great Spilsbury? The very fact that so many eminent doctors had been prepared to argue against Sir Bernard casts doubts over the case wherever it is argued by experts to this day.

Does it constitute a reasonable doubt as to Thorne's guilt? Or was the evidence against him so damning that any other verdict than 'guilty' was unthinkable?

I was in court at the time, and I am still not sure. And I, for one, would not like to bet how the verdict would have gone today.

# 2  Furnace

Some murders are easy enough to solve. We call them 'open-and-shut' cases in newspaper jargon, and they rarely make more than a few paragraphs in the crime reporter's notebook.

Others are ingeniously planned and executed. It is these that set the pulse racing when the hunt is on, and live in the memory long after each piece in the jigsaw has been slotted into place.

Such a murder was the Furnace Case.

It was first uncovered, not because of public alarm or hue and cry, but because of a 'hunch', that sixth sense telling a man of long experience that something that appeared straightforward on the surface did not *feel* right.

To almost all of us, the finding of a note beside a charred body in a burned-out builder's shed at Hawley Crescent, in Camden Town, on the night of 3 January, 1933, looked like a simple case of suicide.

The note seemed explicit enough:

> 'Goodbye all. No work. No money.
>         Sam J. Furnace.'

That note did not satisfy my old friend Dr. Bentley Purchase, then Coroner for Camden Town. It looked all too pat.

'I never *heard* of a man sitting on a stool and waiting to be burned to death,' he said at the post-mortem. 'Turn the body over.'

He examined the corpse carefully and closely. Sure enough there was evidence of foul play: a bullet hole high in the back of the badly burned flesh. Once again I was plunged into the world of murder. This one was brilliantly staged by the killer, whose idea was to 'die' himself and start a new life on the proceeds.

Samuel James Furnace had been around, as they say. In 1933 he was a smalltime builder and decorator. Over the years he had been a ship's steward, a soldier in the Rifle Brigade, and a member of the Black and Tans serving in Ireland. Now he was thirty-nine and short of cash.

On the night of Tuesday, 3 January, a man called Wynne, who lived at 30 Hawley Crescent, called the Fire Brigade and reported a shed ablaze in his yard.

The shed was rented by Sam Furnace, jobbing builder. While Mr. Wynne summoned the fire brigade, a friend of his —using buckets of water—managed to contain the blaze. When the firemen arrived they found, inside, the body of a man sitting on a stool by an office desk. The fire had been fiercest by the stool. Both body and clothing were badly burned. A fresh examination of the premises next morning led to the discovery of the note, which had miraculously escaped the flames.

It looked like a clear case of Sam Furnace killing himself, and destroying the premises, by fire. Two of his relatives called at the mortuary and positively identified the body. There it was: another open-and-shut case. And, at first sight, not even a murder.

When his examination revealed a bullet wound that could not have been self-inflicted, Dr. Purchase informed the police. Det. Superintendent George Cornish, a first-class police officer, who was already working on another murder in his 'manor' or district, took over.

The Yard sent another top man, Detective Chief Inspector Yandell, to aid the inquiry. Cornish and Yandell made a formidable team. They set about their investigation methodically and patiently.

They found a charred overcoat in the shed with what appeared to be a bullet hole in the left shoulder. They soon matched it, for the jacket found on the partly-burned body bore a similar hole, into the back of the left shoulder.

At first, Cornish and Yandell believed they were looking for clues to the identity of the man who murdered Sam Furnace. Now, they were not so sure.

Inside the jacket they found the remains of a Post Office savings book, bearing the name *Walter Spatchett*. It had been through the fire; it had been soaked with water afterwards: it was charred and yellowed and stained, but that much was still decipherable.

Who was Walter Spatchett? 'I want to know everything there is to know about this man Spatchett,' said Cornish to the Murder Squad. From the reports they sent back, a fascinating new picture arose.

Walter Spatchett was a rent collector. He had been reported missing on the day before the fire in Hawley Crescent. He had disappeared on a Monday, the busiest day of the week for a rent collector. But only half the amount of money he would normally have collected on a Monday had been banked. The balance—about £45—was missing. In no way did that fit in with the picture of a man absconding with the firm's money: why would he take only half and bank the rest?

Spatchett's father and brother were taken to the mortuary by Cornish, where they identified the body as Walter's—and the clothing.

One body, but *two* 'positive' and quite genuine identifications!

It had been identified as that of Furnace by his brother, his father-in-law and by two personal friends. They recognised its high cheek bones, the shape of the forehead, a slight physical deformity—and the fountain pen in the charred jacket.

Now it was just as positively identified as that of Walter Spatchett by Spatchett's relatives and two close friends. They recognised a laundry mark on the collar, the remnants of other clothes, the partly destroyed savings book and a number of partly burned letters.

The Yard men immediately called for medical help to establish identity without doubt. They traced the dentist who had been treating Walter Spatchett. He pointed to a misshapen tooth in the fire-seared and physically unrecognisable head.

'That,' he said positively, 'is the tooth of Walter Spatchett.'

As every policeman knows, teeth cannot be destroyed by fire. The flames, instead of continuing the normal course of destruction, merely harden the enamel.

Soon the detectives learned that Furnace had once worked for the same employers as Spatchett. That the men knew each other well, and regularly met for a game of billiards.

A large-scale hunt for Furnace began. Scotland Yard issued this appeal:

'The police are anxious to trace Samuel James Furnace, in connection with the discovery of the body of a man on 3 January, 1933, in a builder's shed at Hawley Crescent, Camden Town.

'It is known that Furnace has been a ship's steward, and has served with the Rifle Brigade and with the Black and Tans.

'He may be endeavouring to obtain employment in the decorating trade or in the Mercantile Marine. He may also endeavour to leave the country.

'Any person with information is requested to communicate with the nearest police station.'

Then came a complete description of the wanted man, even details of his war wounds.

This is what Furnace looked like:

'Height 5ft. 10½in., fair complexion, fair hair (thin in front). Hazel eyes, full face and square jaw, tooth missing upper front jaw.

'Gun-shot wound scars left leg and both arms. Long scar showing marks of 13 stitches on right arm.

'Dressed in navy blue suit, new bright blue shirt and collar, light brown fully belted overcoat, grey trilby hat with blue band and straight brim tilted over right eye, light brown socks, black shoes.

'He may be wearing Discharged Serviceman's badge (silver) on right lapel of overcoat.'

That was a massively detailed description. Someone in the Murder Squad had been doing routine 'homework' with great doggedness and patience.

A watch was clamped on all docks, railway stations and airfields. Nowadays a watch on airports would be automatic. It was a little different then: this actually became the first murder hunt in which Scotland Yard used aircraft to search for a wanted man. The police showed relentless energy and resource in the hunt for Furnace: I still find the pace of inquiry and the concentration of forces impressive.

While they waited patiently for their quarry to be flushed out of hiding, I spoke daily to the detectives who built up this mental picture of the actual murder.

They came to the conclusion that Furnace had met Spatchett by appointment—to play billiards, maybe—and then, on some pretext, lured him into the Hawley Crescent shed. There he shot him through the back, robbed him and concealed the body on the premises until next day, when the 'suicide by fire' was to be staged.

They learned that, on the night of the murder, Furnace had made a point of calling at the billiard hall and asking for his friend Spatchett. And that after leaving a message—for the man he already knew to be dead—he went home and stayed near the radio, ready in case the news of the murder should break. Next day he set fire to the shed, planted the 'suicide note' and vanished.

Furnace had by now failed in the two principal aims of his murder plan:

1. to fool the police into believing the body in the shed was his own;

2. to ensure that his wife and family, to whom he was

devoted, would benefit from a life insurance policy while he masqueraded under another name.

The family, incidentally, where wholly innocent of the plan. Furnace never intended that his wife should suffer from his 'suicide'. With that in mind, he had taken out a special insurance policy on his life, worth £1,000 down and £100 a month for eighteen years, a sizable sum in those days.

It contained the customary clause, rendering it void if the insurer committed suicide within twelve months. Conveniently, the charred and unrecognisable body of 'Furnace' was found thirteen months and two days after forms had been signed.

Furnace came within a hair's-breadth of being caught, with the body, before he could destroy any of the evidence by fire. All he could manage during that first, nerve-racking twenty-four hours was to swathe the body in an old cement sack and jam it under his desk in the shed.

During the day, a labourer called in, looking for work. He sat down opposite Furnace, stretched his legs out—and felt the bulky package under the desk.

'What have you got there?' he asked.

No emotion showed on Furnace's face as he answered. 'Oh, only some cement and stuff I've just bought,' he said casually.

Question and answer passed off without comment. I have never had any doubt in my own mind that there would have been a second murder that day if the labourer had proved too inquisitive!

With continuing newspaper publicity, results began to come in. On 6 January, a couple living in the Regent's Park area reported to the police that a man answering Furnace's description had lodged with them under the name of 'Rogers'.

After staying two days he left, saying he was going to visit a brother in Southend. He left a suit and a bag of tools behind him. Then came a telegram, from *Southend* saying 'Brother ill. Re-let room. Returning Monday. R. Rogers'.

'Mr. Rogers' never returned, which was as well for him. The

suit left behind was positively identified as one owned by Furnace and worn by him on the day Spatchett had died.

The clues to Southend as his new hiding place looked promising. The manhunt now concentrated on the seaside town and its surrounds. The first 'planes to be used in British crime detection droned over the lonely Essex marshes. Murder Squad men ceaselessly patrolled the streets, memorising that detailed description of Sam Furnace. Systematic calls began on the landladies of the town: a monumental task.

Suddenly, a shop keeper reported selling a trench coat to a man answering the Furnace description. That day the BBC broadcast this new Yard message:

'Samuel James Furnace, wanted for the wilful murder of Walter Spatchett, whose dead body was found on 3 January after a fire in a shed at Hawley Crescent, N.W. Since Furnace left home, he has purchased a light double-breasted trench coat with sliding belt. . . .

'It is urgently requested that anyone prepared to take male lodgers, particularly at quiet apartment houses, will keep a lookout for this man and if seen communicate with the nearest police station.

'Furnace, who takes rooms under a false name, is believed to be in possession of a service revolver, without a holster. He may endeavour to board a ship.'

With the hunt at its height, the police under Cornish and Yandell decided to use one more ploy to tighten the screw.

When Scotland Yard so demands, the postal authorities in Britain are empowered to put a 'stop' on letters to any given list of addresses. The letters are intercepted, handed to Yard men who open and read them, note the contents, re-seal the letters and put them back to be posted in the normal way. It takes an expert to tell that the mail has been tampered with.

Cornish ordered a 'stop' on letters to all relatives of Samuel Furnace. It was a shrewd decision: on 14 January it paid off.

A letter signed 'H. Farmer' came—from Southend—to Mr. Charles Tuckfield, a brother-in-law of the wanted man. It read:

Dear Charlie,

Just a line to you in hope that I shall be able to see a friend before I end it all. I am writing to you because I know they will watch May [Furnace's wife] for a long time.

'I am at Southend, quite near the station, making out I have been ill with the 'flu. So have been able to stay in all the week. I am far from well through want of sleep. I don't think I have slept one hour since the accident happened. I will tell you all about it when I see you. Now what I want you to do is not for me, but for May and the kiddies.

'My days are numbered. I want you to come down Sunday, on your own, please. Catch the 10.35 from Harringay Park, that will get you down to Southend at 12.8.

'Come out of the station, walk straight across the road and down the opposite side. Walk on the left side.

'I will see you. I am not giving my address in case you are followed. Just walk slowly down. If you come will you bring me 15½in. shirt and two collars, any colour will do. Also one pair of socks, dark ones, and one comb. I think that is all now.

'Best of luck. Mine is gone.

H. Farmer.'

Mr. Tuckfield, the brother-in-law, went straight to the police with that letter. It cannot have been an easy thing for him to do. The irony is, he never knew the police already knew its contents and were acting on them. Whitegate Road, Southend, was already under constant observation.

Leading the watchers was a police inspector, playing the violin. Det. Inspector King, from the Yard, happened to be a keen amateur fiddler—and few artists have ever made a more dramatic public entrance. Remember, the police believed Furnace still to be armed, and desperate. By process of elimination, they thought they knew the house he was in.

Outside, up and down for two days, wandered the Murder Squad's first working violinist. If King's repertoire was limited, his energy was boundless. The good citizens—and bad!—of Whitegate Road were given *O Sole Mio, The Lost Chord* and all the world war pop songs like *Tipperary* and *Pack up your troubles* from morning till night, and this was one time when complaints to the police would fall on deaf ears. As it happened, Furnace suspected nothing. King was to have his leg pulled for years afterwards.

Sunday came. The 10.35 from Harringay arrived on time, and Mr. Tuckfield the brother-in-law—who had been told to go ahead and keep the rendezvous—began what must have been the longest walk of his life, along the left-hand side of Whitegate Road.

Suddenly a lace curtain in one window was pushed aside. A piece of white paper bearing the letters 'S A M' was then pushed against the pane.

Mr. Tuckfield turned, walked towards the front door. There was no need to knock. It opened on the instant he drew level. And as soon as both men were inside the house, Furnace blurted out his version of 'the accident'.

Spatchett, he said, was in his office and had seen the revolver. He picked it up, in spite of warnings by Furnace that it was loaded. As it was handed back, Spatchett had jerked open the door. It struck Furnace's hand and caused the gun to go off. Spatchett fell, dead.

It was a story that could never have held water in a court of law. The police knew too much: but Furnace, not knowing how much they knew, babbled on.

The men spoke, wretchedly, for an hour or more. Finally Sam Furnace asked Mr. Tuckfield to go out and buy him some cigarettes. As soon as he was clear of the house and its windows, the Yard men closed on Tuckfield and asked the vital question: 'Has he still got the gun?'

'No,' answered the brother-in-law. 'He says he threw it into the canal at Camden Town.'

Still wary, the detectives closed in quietly and quickly at the back of the house. First Cornish went in, then Yandell, then a detective inspector called Ockey.

None of them could be sure if Furnace was armed or not: they could only hope Mr. Tuckfield was right. So they decided to rush in and overpower him before he could grasp what was happening. They tiptoed down the hallway and positioned themselves. They persuaded the landlady—busy with Sunday dinner—to knock on the door and push it open, saying 'Did you call?' She did so. At that second they ran in and seized Furnace who sat reading by the fire. He was an Edgar Wallace fan, and Cornish told me later that the book was a Wallace thriller, *Traitor's Gate*.

Furnace put up no resistance. On the way back to the police station at Kentish Town, he stopped the police car and showed his captors the spot where he had thrown away the revolver.

Inside the station he was cautioned and charged. He made a statement, repeating the 'accident' story. He told them how he had lost his head once he realised Spatchett was dead, threw the gun away and went home.

Next day, 'I returned to the shop about 2 p.m. to set it on fire. I sat there for some time. I went out into Kentish Town road and met one of my workmen. I returned to the shop later.

'I put the body in the office chair, pouring over it oil and spirits. I screwed up a lot of paper on the floor, and set a candle, which I lit, in the middle of it. I shut the office door. I came outside, and pulled the outer door to, locking it.'

Oddly, Furnace did not appear to be downhearted. They said later that he had the air of a man confident of cheating the hangman. And cheat him he did.

A search of his clothing failed to reveal a small phial sewn into the lining of his overcoat. In the early hours of that exceptionally cold night in January, Sam Furnace asked the policeman who had just come on duty outside his cell if he could have the coat as he felt so cold, and wanted to sleep.

As soon as he slipped the coat on, he worked the phial—of poison—free and swallowed the contents. The doctors tried but failed to save him for the hangman. Samuel James Furnace died twenty-four hours later, in agony.

On 20 January, the coroner's jury found him guilty of the wilful murder of Walter Spatchett.

The open-and-shut story of apparent suicide in a hut remained a real-life thriller, right to the end. It also provided a chilling postscript.

As Spatchett's relatives went through his belongings in the final, melancholy chores they discovered a Christmas card sent by Furnace the year before. It was captioned 'The Friendly Light'. On the front was a snow-covered cottage. Reflected in its windows was the bright red glow of a fire.

I have often wondered: did the first inkling of murder come on the night he bought that card?

# 3  The Biggest Liar

On 21 October, 1949, farm hand Sidney Tiffin was out wild-fowling on the bleak and lonely Dengie Marshes, off the Essex coast. It was a little after midday.

There was no sign of duck, and as he rose to move to a fresh hide, Tiffin noticed a bundle floating in the water. It was wrapped in felt and bound by rope. But Mr. Tiffin—who was duckshooting, not beachcombing—left it undisturbed.

Half an hour later it came bobbing by again, close in, as though pleading to be investigated. This time he dragged the parcel in, cut the ropes and looked inside. There he saw the torso of a man, hands bound behind and held by a leather strap.

The wildfowler kept a level head. He drove a wooden stake into the shallows, bound the right hand of the *thing* to it, and then waded back across the marshes to tell the police of his dreadful find. To get to a telephone, to guide the police back through that wild marshland, took many hours. It was dark when they found the stake, with the body tethered to it.

Next morning the parcel was found to hold a body, minus head and legs. It was taken to the mortuary at Chelmsford. The Essex CID immediately informed the Yard. The late Professor Francis Camps, the eminent pathologist and a friend of mine for many years, was called to help inquiries.

Grim and unpleasant though it must be, the work of such men is crime detection at its purest and most sophisticated.

Here the police presented Camps with a dripping, headless, legless human trunk newly fished from the marshes and said, in effect: 'Tell us who he is and how he died.'

The murderer, whoever he or she was, seemed to have eased the burden in one respect, by leaving the hands intact. If the victim had a previous criminal record, it would be only a matter of time before identity was established beyond all doubt.

Fingerprint expert Det. Chief Superintendent Fred Cherrill, a man whose reputation was a household word with police forces throughout the world, stood by at Scotland Yard as the telltale skin fragments were rushed from Chelmsford.

If there was no past record, then all depended on Camps. He set to work in typical fashion: quiet; quick but never hasty; shrewd in observation and suggestion.

He pronounced the unknown man well-fed, running to obesity. He would have been small—about 5ft. 7in. in height. Estimated overall weight at death, 13 stone 6 lbs.

From the state of the body, Camps was able to tell the Murder Squad it had been approximately twenty-one days in the water; that it was not more than forty-eight hours dead when dumped into the marshes; and that, although there was no head to guide his inquiry, it looked as though the victim had been stabbed to death. There were five separate stab wounds on the front of the chest alone.

From his examination of body and clothing fragments, Dr. Camps was able to describe the weapon used. Double edged, about one inch wide and at least four inches long. And it looked to Camps as if the man was standing up, or perhaps sitting up, when death came. He could tell the police the knife struck from right to left and, most likely, the murderer rained blows in quick succession.

So, that first night in the mortuary, the police already had an idea of the build and height of their dead man, a picture of the moment of death, a description of the murder weapon, and they knew he had been dismembered within forty-eight hours or so of the knife attack and that the body had lain a maximum of three weeks in the offshore marshes before discovery.

Dr. Camps also found the unknown victim had consumed the equivalent of *eight* double scotches (or brandies) before he died. This vital point, which was never raised by the prosecution at the trial, helped to save the killer's life, as I shall show.

Back at the Yard, and working with equal speed and expertise, Cherrill was able to report that their man was named Stanley Setty, an Iraqi-born Warren Street car dealer whose record showed he had once been convicted for a bankruptcy offence. First-class teamwork!

Setty had been reported missing on 5 October. He was last seen alive, by a relative, at about 5.30 p.m. on 4 October, driving his cream Citroen car along Great Portland Street. His sister had also seen him a little while earlier, and it was she who reported her brother missing on the 5th. She was insistent that something untoward had happened, as he was a man of regular and unchangeable habit.

His empty car had been found by the police, outside his garage in Cambridge Terrace Mews, key in the ignition switch.

Inquiries by Det. Chief Inspector Jamieson of Albany Street station revealed that Setty had been handed £1,000 in five pound notes for a car deal the day before he vanished. The bank cashier was able to give the police a complete list of the numbers of those fivers. Setty's family had in fact offered a reward of £1,000 for news of the missing man. It had brought no response.

Now here *was* Setty, sixty miles from home, floating dead and dismembered in the Essex marshes. The investigation into his murder was to prove one of the most bizarre and ghoulish in which I was ever involved. It ended with the killer being found 'not guilty' of Setty's murder. And with the killer—who knew no man can be tried twice on the same murder charge—walking into my office and trying to sell me the inside story of his 'perfect' crime!

But to get back to the Chelmsford mortuary, where the hunt started. . . .

Camps found that Setty's blood group was 'O'. Since he must have lost blood in the knife attack and later, here was a helpful clue if and when the place of death was traced.

According to Camps, dismemberment had been carried out by a person with some knowledge of how to cut up meat or flesh, but *not* medical knowledge. The arms had been pinioned after death and the trunk tied up in a parcel which would have measured at least 31in. by 17in. by 6in. and its dry weight would have been 110 lbs, i.e., big and bulky and very likely to have been seen in transit by innocent passers by. And after death, somehow, the body had been crushed, pulverised, breaking the ribs, in a manner *consistent with a fall from considerable height*.

Dr. Camps was making crime history in Britain: unravelling the first case of disposal of a body by dumping it, section by section, into the sea from an aeroplane.

The news of the find in the marshes was prominently given in every newspaper. I can never emphasise too strongly how vital a part newspapers play in crime detection. Without them (and, of course, television) detective work would at all times be severely hampered. In this case, the newspaper publicity led the police directly to the murderer.

Following the stories about the body in Dengie Marshes, a telephone call was made to the police from Elstree aerodrome. The caller said that on 5 October, a man named Hume had hired an Auster (a small light plane) at Elstree. When he arrived to pilot it, he parked his car and carried two parcels from it to the aircraft. He placed one in the back seat of the plane, the other in the pilot's seat.

My own guess—with hindsight—was that this was Hume suffering from a severe attack of the 'jitters'. It was a blunder, the sort of mistake that cannot fail to draw attention from the staff at such a small airfield. Somebody spotted it and straightway told Hume he would have to move it before he could climb in and start up.

C

A fitter named Bill Davey told Hume, who then moved the parcel to the co-pilot's seat. A small incident but it stuck in Davey's mind, and he was later able to describe the parcels: one he said was 'sort of square', the other was bulky and 'about two to three feet long'.

The Murder Squad team was jubilant when this information came through. Time is vital in getting any investigation going before the trail gets cold. Now all the hard work, all the brilliant deductions, were paying off with really handsome speed.

Further inquiries showed that the man called Hume had landed at Southend at 6.30 p.m. minus the parcels. Furthermore he landed in such a dangerous manner, nearly colliding with another aircraft, that everyone at the field noted the time, date and every relevant detail of his arrival. They remembered Hume had tried and failed to get another pilot to fly him back to Elstree, and that eventually he had left the plane at Southend that night and taken a taxi back to Finchley.

He was back again at Southend next day, with more parcels which he loaded from the car into the Auster. He took off between three and four o'clock that afternoon and landed again (this time at Gravesend) at 5.45 p.m. Without any parcels. Instead the Auster this time had on board a travelling rug and a bag. Hume took another taxi to Golders Green.

Once all this was reported, Dr. H. S. Holden, another pathologist working with Dr. Camps, went down to Elstree and examined the aircraft. He found traces of blood behind the co-pilot's seat.

The Murder Squad decided it was high time to pick up Mr. Hume for questioning about the trips and the parcels. On Wednesday, 26 October, Chief Inspector Jamieson called on Hume at his flat in Finchley Road, Golders Green, and escorted him to Albany Street police station.

At first Hume denied he knew anything about Setty's disappearance or anything about parcels in the Auster. Once he realised how much the police knew, he changed his tune. I repeat much of his statement here to show how it now held the basis of an alibi good enough to withstand cross-examination in a high court trial on a capital charge.

'I am a married man and live with my wife Cynthia and daughter aged three months at Golders Green,' he began.

'I served for eighteen months in the RAF during the war, and had a few hours' instruction in flying, and about nine months ago I joined the United Services Flying Club. I was eventually able to fly solo, but I have had only one hour's instruction in map reading, and I should have difficulty in finding my bearings in poor visibility.

'During the last three years I have had dealings with motor dealers in Warren Street, including a Mr. Salvadori and a Mr. Manfield and I told them I could fly a plane, and romanced about my capabilities as a pilot.

'On occasions I had been asked if I could fly people to Italy and Belgium, and I met in Salvadori's office a man I know as Mac or Max, about thirty-five years of age, 5ft. 10–11in. tall, heavily built, clean shaven with a fresh complexion, fair hair parted in the centre and brushed right back. He usually wears suède brogue shoes and a large stone ring on the right hand.

'On Friday, 30 September I was in Salvadori's office when I met this man Mac again, and he asked me if I was the flying smuggler, and I said "yes". He invited me to have a cup of tea and introduced me to a man called Gree or Green.' Hume then gave a description of this new central figure in his alibi. 'He asked me if I should like to make some money, and I gave him my phone number.'

Hume told the police how Mac phoned at 10 a.m. on 5 October and told him to get a plane.

Then, said Hume, 'between 2 p.m. and 3 p.m., Mac, Gree and a man called Boy'—here another detailed description flowed from Hume's lips—'came to my flat. Gree and Boy were each carrying a parcel. He said something about forged petrol coupons and wanting to get rid of the plates and presses, and said he wanted them dumped.'

'They showed me a gun and gave me ten £5 notes. I was

impressed by the three men I had to take up the plates and throw them into the English Channel. Before leaving my flat Mac said "We will call round about eight to a quarter past eight tonight and pay you another £50."

'I would describe the parcels, the one Boy brought was a Heinz Baked Beans box, about 15in. by 15in. by 15in., completely covered by cardboard and securely roped. The other parcel was 2ft. 6in. long and about 2ft. thick and round. It was heavy and when I squeezed it with my fingers it had a soft feeling, and when I lifted the parcel it did not bend or sag. It was fairly heavy. I did not see any dry or wet stains, or moisture, on these packages.

'Whilst the parcels were in my house and after the men left, I put them in a cupboard in the kitchen of my flat. I would not know if any staining had been left on the floor of my cupboard. I feel sure that my wife did not see the parcels at any time whilst they were in the flat.'

He also told how he eventually put the parcels in a hired car, paid (in £5 notes) for the plane hire at Elstree airport, and took off about four-thirty in the afternoon.

'I flew towards Southend, reached the pier and straight out to sea and continued for a quarter of an hour towards the Kent coast.

'Just before I turned to the right, I opened the door on the pilot's side of the 'plane with both hands, and held the controls with my knees. After I got the door open, I was able to hold it open against air resistance and throw both parcels out of the plane and into the sea. I was then flying about 1,000 feet and would estimate I was about four to five miles from the end of Southend pier.'

He flew back to Southend and hired a cab to take him to Golders Green. He paid—with another fiver—and told the driver 'keep the change', a tip of £1.

As he walked towards the door of his flat, said Hume, Mac came towards him. He led Hume across the road where Gree and Boy were waiting, with another 'bulky package' in their car. They told Hume they wanted him to drop it into the sea that night. Hume said he told them it was 'too big to get into the 'plane'.

Eventually it was agreed he could dump it next day. So Mac and Boy carried the parcel upstairs into his flat and put it in the far kitchen cupboard. He ordered a hire car to take him back to Elstree.

'During the morning, I think about eleven, with the help of an employee from the carhire firm I carried the bundle downstairs and placed it in the car.

'While I was taking it downstairs, it made a gurgling noise. I thought it was a human body, that of a small or young person. It crossed my mind that the package may have contained Setty's body, as I had read in the papers that morning that he was missing. I knew Stanley Setty because I had sold him a Pontiac two years ago, for £200.'

Next in his statement, Hume told his own story of the second macabre air journey.

'I had got one of the ground staff to help me put the parcel in the upright position. When I tried to drop the parcel I had difficulty, but by pushing the package against the door, I managed to get it open.

'I let go of the controls, and it went into a vertical turn and the parcel fell out into the sea. I lost my way and landed in a ploughed field at Faversham, Kent. Someone gave the propeller a swing for me, and I took off and landed at Gravesend, where I left the plane as it was too dark. . . .'

Later in the statement Hume said: 'As far as I can remember, on Friday, 7 October, having seen in the paper the numbers of the £5 notes which were reported as having been in Setty's possession when he disappeared, I checked these with notes given me by Boy and found that four of these notes were identical.'

He said he disposed of the money he was paid in the following manner:

'£80 in £5 notes to my wife, who put £40 into the Post

Office savings account of our baby, and £40 into her own
account;

'£5 at Fortnum and Masons for an address book;

'£5 at a shop in the Burlington Arcade for a set of scissors
in a red leather case;

'Two £5 notes to a tobacconist and confectioners in the
Edgware Road.'

Hume said next that Boy rang him on Sunday, 23 October,
when he was reading in the papers that part of Setty's body
had been found in Essex. Boy had said 'I hope you are not
getting any views about getting squeamish and claiming any
reward—you have a wife and baby.'

'I said "I presume I am in it as deep as you are, for £150
at that." ' And Hume claimed he had never heard since from
Mac, Gree or Boy.

We know now this statement was lying in so many places. I
doubt if anyone (outside the jury!) accepted it at much more
than face value at the time. But I have quoted it fully here
because it shows—in its very speed of invention and plaus-
ibility—just how clever and resourceful a liar Hume was. He
stuck to the story of Mac, Gree and Boy throughout his trial
and their wholly fictitious characters saved him from the
rope.

Very considerable efforts were made by the police to exploit
its weaknesses. A number of bloodstains were found in Hume's
flat—Group O, Setty's blood group. Alas, 42 per cent of the
whole population of this country is also Group O.

They interviewed the Humes' part-time daily help. She told
them how she went to clean the flat on 5 October, to find that
the sitting room carpet had been removed. She said Hume told
her he had washed it but as his own efforts had not been
'satisfactory' he had then sent it to the cleaners. He had added
that he felt, while he was at it, he would have the floor surround stained—plus the surround in the dining room. Then
he had told her he was going into the kitchen for an hour and
did not want to be disturbed. She saw him go out of the flat

soon after four o'clock that afternoon carrying some brown paper parcels.

They found another witness who said Hume had asked him to sharpen a carving knife around 1 p.m. that same day. He also said Hume had seemed to be in a hurry and took the knife away unfinished after only a 'rough grind'. There was also the painter who stained the floors. He had actually helped Hume carry the big parcel downstairs and put it into the car.

Now while the initial work by the Murder Squad, coupled with the research by Dr. Camps and his staff, were of the highest quality in this case I have always felt the prosecution left loopholes in its presentation that enabled Hume to get away with a comparatively light sentence as accessory.

No evidence was produced in court to link Hume with the initial buying of felt and rope that made the parcels in which Setty's remains were wrapped. This vital point would have wrecked his alibi wherein Mac, Gree and Boy first produced the parcels and carried them into his flat.

Another point scored by the defence came with the evidence of pathologist Dr. Donald Teare. He said that the absence of wounds on Setty's hands (which, you remember, were found intact) were consistent with the theory that he was held by someone while being stabbed. In other words, credibility for Hume's story of Mac, Gree and Boy.

But no evidence was called by the Crown to show that Dr. Camps' examination of the torso had shown Setty had consumed the equivalent of eight double whiskies or brandies at the time of death. Enough to render most men incapable of defending themselves against attack!

The defence of course put up a magnificent winning fight for their client's life. Hume was a supreme liar, the biggest and best I have ever met in a lifetime of crime coverage. Add these points to vital loopholes in the prosecution case, throw in all the unique legal drama that attended the hearing (the original judge falling ill, the jury disagreeing) and there could be only one answer.

Hume was acquitted of murder. No man in my opinion was ever luckier to draw twelve years as accessory after the fact. I liked none of it, but it is my business to report, not to judge.

I weighed him up in my own mind during the trial as a 'wide boy', a typical criminal product of the postwar period, ex-Forces and not lacking in resource (I thought of that terrifying flight in the Auster, when the body jammed in the half open door and the plane went into its spin); callous, glib, brazenly dishonest ('the flying smuggler'); and a liar. I thought of the fivers, the staining of the floors, the impatience for the knife to be sharpened and had no doubts myself he was entirely capable of and responsible for the murder of car dealer Stanley Setty.

I had no idea I would ever see him again.

Good behaviour in prison earned him maximum remission, and he was released on 1 February, 1958. Five days later, on the morning of the 6th, damned if he didn't enter my office at the *Daily Express,* unrepentant, grinning, brazen as ever—to confess to the murder of Stanley Setty!

# 4  Hume and Timothy Evans

I have seen many murderers in the dock and my feelings for all of them are much the same. By their act they put themselves beyond the pale and it matters not one jot or tittle to me that they may have killed for passion or greed. Any sympathies I may have are always reserved for the victim. My admiration is reserved for the devoted, poorly paid detective who overcomes every difficulty and brings the criminal to book. My especial loathing is of the sex-killer of children.

Having said all that, I will now add that of all the killers I have met, Hume was the one who most disgusted me.

On 6 February, 1958, the day he walked into my office and confessed to the murder of Stanley Setty, Hume was positively smirking with pleasure at the way in which he had outwitted society.

Still lying—I feel it in my bones we still have not heard all the story behind the Setty murder; entirely without remorse or pity for his victim; with his pudgy white face alight with enjoyment at the prospect of making money out of murder, Hume revolted me. He knew he could never be tried again for the crime. So now, five days out of prison, he was coolly asking for thousands of pounds (he was eventually paid £10,000 by another newspaper) for the 'real story' of how he did the murder, of how he had fooled the court with his invented characters called Mac, Gree and Boy.

I told him my newspaper would not bid for this type of

story. But I broke the news quietly enough and gave him no
hint of my personal feelings. I had my own sources of information concerning Mr. Hume, and there was one chapter in his
life I dearly wanted to know more about: the time he spent
with fellow-murderer Timothy Evans in the hospital wing of
Brixton Prison.

The office boy who brought us cups of tea that morning
could not take his eyes off Hume and he was something to
look at. Brilliantined black hair curled untidily over his prison-
white face. His eyes glowed in his head as he spoke about
the 'perfect murder'. He wriggled and fidgeted in his chair, and
kept swinging round as though to make sure no-one eaves-
dropped on our conversation. He looked what he was: an
evil, sly and highly dangerous animal.

I tried my best to make him feel important and said: 'Sorry.
I'm afraid my editor would say it is not our type of journalism.'

As he made to leave, I said: 'There is something you can
tell me. What on earth did you do that day in Brixton to make
Timothy Evans withdraw his confession to those two murders
at 10 Rillington Place?'

As everyone knows, young Evans had shared that notorious
address with the mass murderer John Reginald Christie. He
was hanged in 1950 for the murder of his baby daughter and
had at one time also admitted strangling his nineteen-year-
old wife. The Evans case is a *cause célèbre*. Debate has raged
ever since over his hanging: did he kill the child, did he kill
or take part in the killing of his wife? Would Evans have been
hanged if the jury had known Christie was a necrophiliac
murderer himself?

To my mind, there is one damning piece of evidence against
Evans. At the time of his arrest he told one of the CID men
investigating the case:

'After I killed my wife, I took the wedding ring off her
finger and sold it for six shillings in Merthyr.' And sure enough,
when the Murder Squad called at the jeweller's shop in the
Welsh town to check on his story, there was the ring.

I believe, as did the police investigating the murder, that placed Evans on the spot at the time his wife was killed. All those people who are against capital punishment—and they are fully entitled to their views, since endorsed by Parliament in a free vote—have never accepted Evans' guilt.

Now, sitting at my desk in the office, was the one man who might know the answer. That was why I put the question to Hume. How had he persuaded Evans to withdraw his confession? His reply was typical. Hume was plain anti-law-and-order. 'I thought he was stupid to have made all those confessions to the police. I told him to admit nothing in court, just to think out his best story and stick to it.'

Hume then went on to say Evans had told him of the arrangement he had with Christie for disposing of Mrs. Evans. And that Christie had murdered her and also the child. 'It was because the kid kept crying,' Evans told Hume.

Evans said that Christie had gone into a bedroom and strangled the child with a piece of rag while he—Evans— 'looked on'.

How much reliance can one put on Hume's version?

Hume told me: 'When Evans came in I put him down as a "flash boy". He was wearing high-buckle shoes and a camel-hair coat. I thought he was a bit of an idiot and needed some advice. So I told him to pick out the best story and stick to it —*blame everyone but himself.*'

Hume later refused to testify at the Scott Henderson inquiry into the Evans case. He most certainly had his own doubts about Evans' story, as told in Brixton prison, as he himself told me that morning after his release: 'I found that bit about the kid especially hard to swallow.'

If Hume was telling the truth, that Evans revealed how he had arranged with Christie for the disposal of his wife and then watched as Christie strangled his child 'because the kid kept on crying', many people may feel he was properly hanged in any event.

If you believe nothing Hume said, and I repeat, he was the

biggest liar I ever met, then—like me—you are forced to weigh those damning words he told the detective about how he took the wedding ring off his dead wife's finger, where he sold it and how much he got for it. I personally have searched my conscience and still maintain Timothy Evans was rightly hanged.

Ironically, Hume was back in prison—and on a murder charge—exactly one year after he was freed in this country. After carrying out armed bank raids in London he flew to Switzerland. On 30 January, 1959, he held up a bank in Zürich and got away with a miserable £17 in silver.

While making his escape he shot fifty-year-old Arthur Maag, a taxi driver who tried to stop him. Maag died: the next day Hume was charged with his murder. He is now serving hard labour for life in the Regensdorf Jail in Switzerland. Few people visit him. He spends most of his time painting animals, from memory. A caged wild animal painting those that are free.

# 5   Smoke Clings to the Hair

It is a joy to see a good copper at work. Their pay is disgrace-fully low for the responsibility they bear. Their hours are long, for there can never be enough policemen to go round in this wicked world. Many of them work in conditions inside police stations which would cause an instant strike on the factory floor. Most are unknown to the general public they serve: usually only the police of fiction novels enjoy household names.

I doubt, for instance, if you have ever heard of Chief Inspec-tor Hambrook of Scotland Yard. I first met him in 1929. He solved a murder at Margate by combining infinite patience with rare astuteness and impressed me mightily in the process. It was a joy to watch him at work.

In October 1929 a man walked into the post office at Mar-gate and handed in a London-bound telegram which read simply: *Extremely muddy water down here.* It was nothing to do with the conditions for bathing at that bracing resort. It signalled the beginning of a murder investigation—and the call for Hambrook to come down and take over.

The telegram was delivered to City solicitor Sir William Charles Crocker and came from one of his insurance investi-gators. He already held a letter from a Margate solicitor who was acting for a client named Mr. Sidney Harry Fox. The letter notified the death of Fox's mother, Mrs. Rosaline Fox, from suffocation and shock following a fire in her room at the

Hotel Metropole; and it formally entered a claim on behalf of Sidney Fox in respect of insurance policies covering such a possibility worth £3,000.

Pinned to the formal letter was an intriguing private memo. It showed that from 1 May of that year until the day of his mother's death, Mr. Fox had taken out a daily insurance policy on her life for no fewer than 167 days out of a possible total of 176.

Strange enough in all conscience. And strange enough to warrant the private investigation Sir William had ordered when you read the further points in this memorandum. That Mr. Fox, for instance, had been 'very anxious' to get a correct definition of the policy's accidental death clause. If his mother drowned in a bath, would *that* be an accident within the meaning of the policy? And he had also wanted to know how he stood if, say, she were poisoned by food in a restaurant?

Now Mrs. Fox had died, the coroner had recorded a verdict of misadventure, and the bereaved son who had made such diligent inquiries into the accident clause was now claiming his £3,000.

Sir William picked up the telephone and asked for Scotland Yard.

As far as anyone knew, the circumstances of Mrs. Fox's death were straightforward enough. She was sixty-three years old. He was a devoted son. They had arrived at the Metropole three weeks earlier, saying they had just returned from a sentimental visit to the graves of two members of their family who had died in the Great War. Sidney Fox was extremely well spoken: so much so there was little comment about their lack of luggage.

Fire broke out in Mrs. Fox's bedroom a week later. It seemed she had been reading an evening paper in front of a lighted gas fire. She had dozed off, the paper had slipped to the floor and caught light. Sidney Fox himself discovered the fire. He could not get into the room because of the smoke. Instead he ran downstairs for help. One guest bravely crawled into the room on his hands and knees, found Mrs. Fox and dragged her out. Another got in and stamped out the flames round the chair in which she had been sitting. Yet another located and turned out the gas fire.

They tried artificial respiration but it was too late to help poor Mrs. Fox. Next day there was an inquest. A local doctor gave his opinion that death was caused by suffocation and a verdict of misadventure was duly recorded. Five days later she was buried in the sleepy village of Great Fransham in Norfolk where she had spent so many years of married life— and a convenient distance from Margate, where the Chief Constable was none too happy about the 'misadventure'.

His suspicions had first been roused following a call from a Margate landlady who had read a newspaper report of the inquest. She had previously let rooms to the Foxes, mother and son, and they had no money to pay her bill. So how, she wanted to know, could they afford rooms in the Metropole? She was sure of one thing: Sidney Fox was not telling the truth when he said he 'had lost all his money' in the blaze in his mother's room.

Another thing nagged at the Chief Constable as persistently as toothache. Fox was sure he had not entered his mother's room. Yet the hotel manager's wife—trying to console him while efforts were made to revive his mother—had stroked his hair in pity as he sat sobbing with grief. And later she remembered vividly how her hands smelled of smoke. She asked the Chief how Sidney Fox could get so much smoke in his hair if he never entered the room?

At the Chief Constable's request, the manager of the Metropole took out a warrant charging Sidney Fox with obtaining food and accommodation by false pretences (an offence they now knew, from the landlady, he had committed before coming to the hotel). It was only a holding charge, a precaution against those deeper suspicions. A policeman brought Fox back from Norwich, where he had been pressing for payment of his insurance claim.

It was ten days after the funeral. Fox was already in custody when Chief Inspector Hambrook came down from the Yard. He had a suspect; he had him inside on a holding charge: now to make the murder charge 'stick'—or set their man free. Reporters and cameramen from Fleet Street flocked into Margate. I set up shop in the same hotel as the Yard team, watching and waiting.

Hambrook was a man of immense patience. 'Let's set the room exactly as it was when the old lady died,' he ordered. To the hotel staff it seemed an impossible task. The room had long been cleaned up and even refurnished. The litter of burned paper and clothing and carpet had been rotting for days somewhere on the Corporation rubbish tip underneath tons of other rubbish since collected and dumped.

The Chief Inspector rounded up a small army of dustmen and detectives. They slogged away and dug for days, sifting the muck, examining each layer with dogged persistence. Finally they found some of Mrs. Fox's charred clothing. And with it, fragments of the same papers that had been burned in the fire.

Fragment by fragment they reconstructed that room. They put the old armchair back in its original position. Then began a series of painstaking experiments. From them Hambrook established that the fire *must* have started beneath that chair. This ruled out the space between chair and fireplace—which would have been the centre of the blaze had it been caused by accident. Now Hambrook began a new series of experiments, with himself and his murder squad as guinea pigs. They lit fires in a room of identical size to Mrs. Fox's hotel bedroom and stayed inside, breathing in smoke with the regular steady intake of a sleeping person.

He found he could not clear his throat outside, so coated were his lungs with soot from the fire. Now if Mrs. Fox *had* died as she slept her lungs would show similar effect. This meant a post mortem. Hambrook applied for exhumation of the body. Early on a November morning Hambrook and the great Sir Bernard Spilsbury arrived at Great Fransham. The coffin was lifted from the grave and carried into an empty village classroom.

Very soon Spilsbury was able to tell Hambrook his suspicions were right. Mrs. Fox had not breathed during the fire. Throat and lungs were clear of soot or any other effect of smoke. Nor was there any trace of carbon monoxide in the blood. Spilsbury found a bruise on the larynx and another on the tongue, suggesting death from strangulation. And he asked Hambrook—'What happened to the old lady's false teeth?' There were none in her head. Yet as she had died Mrs. Fox had bitten deep into her tongue.

Hambrook—who had been called in ten days after the funeral—now went back to Margate and began a search for the missing dentures.

He started questioning the hotel staff. Finally he traced a chambermaid who remembered finding them in a basin as she cleaned up the room after the fire. She was certain she had found them there immediately after the fire. 'That's it,' said Hambrook. 'How could a woman already dead walk across the room and put her teeth into a basin?'

Sidney Fox was tried at Lewes Assize for one of the rarest crimes in the calendar—matricide. There never was much doubt about the verdict although the defence tried hard. Once again the courtroom became a setting for a clash of opinions between the two famous pathologists: Spilsbury for the Crown, Dr. Robert Bronte for the defence.

Spilsbury was unwavering in his conclusion that absence of soot in the dead woman's lungs and of carbon monoxide in her blood proved she was dead before the fire started. Fox was a good witness most of the time. A violent thunderstorm broke soon after he entered the box. Question and answer were given to accompanying claps of thunder and flashes of lightning outside the court. Fox stayed unshaken as he told his story leading up to the outbreak of fire in his mother's bedroom.

D

Then Attorney General Sir William Jowitt nailed him with a series of questions about the fire.

'Did you realise,' he asked Fox, 'when you opened the communicating door that the atmosphere of the room was such as would probably suffocate anybody inside?'

'If I had stayed in three or four moments, *I* should have been suffocated,' answered Sidney Fox.

Attorney General: 'So that you must have been greatly apprehensive for your mother?'

'I was,' said Fox.

Pause.

'Fox, you *closed* the door?'

'It is quite possible I did.'

'Can you explain to me,' said the Attorney General inexorably, 'why it was that you closed the door instead of flinging it wide open?'

Fox hesitated over his reply. 'My explanation for that now,' he said slowly, 'is that the smoke should not spread into the hotel.'

Of course! Fox could not be certain his mother was dead. So he shut her in, hoping the smoke would make doubly sure before the fire was discovered. The verdict was a formality. At four o'clock on that afternoon of Friday, 21 March, 1930, Mr. Justice Rowlatt donned the black cap and sentenced Fox to death. The son who had murdered his mother did not even bother to appeal.

It was a clumsy murder, with the path to the gallows fairly strewn with clues—particularly those persistent questions about accidental death as he took out each policy—yet Sidney Fox came within an ace of success. The local doctor who waived a post mortem and gave death by suffocation to the coroner as cause, very nearly handed that £3,000 to Fox on a plate.

Even that is debatable. Like all similar policies, it contained a clause that stipulated the insured person must be in good health. Rosaline Fox in fact suffered from paralysis agitans.

Be that as it may, I hold the view that Fox's fate was settled the day they called in Hambrook of the Yard. The way he stuck it out in that miserable rubbish tip, day after day, calling on his men for 'just one more try, lads' while he himself never once knew precisely what they were seeking, was something to behold.

# 6   The Classic Crime Picture

Two world wars have changed the whole pattern of murder here in Britain. During them, millions of men were trained in the use of firearms. After each war, a lot of men brought back guns illegally. Today the bank robbery without gunplay is the exception rather than the rule. Policemen are shot down without hesitation by criminals on the run, especially now that the hangman is out of business.

But until the turn of this century, and even up to the beginning of World War 2, murder by shooting was rated a fairly uncommon crime. It was more common in the countryside, where every farmhand had his rabbit gun, than in the big cities, but even there use of the gun for premeditated murder *by the sane person* was rare enough.

It is not hard to see why. The gun is noisy: so noisy that it hinders both secret execution of the crime and undetected getaway. And guns can be too easily identified and traced. Too easily, that is, for the professional criminal.

This was certainly the case even in 1940. Most people were bent on turning guns towards the German enemy rather than on private victims. If you called out any policeman to investigate murder by shooting at that time—how different is it today!—the chances are that the first motive he would look for would be a trifling one. Jealousy, for instance: the most common of all in cases of this kind.

On a sunny afternoon in July 1940 Det. Chief Superintendent Peter Beveridge was called from the Yard to Crittenden, a pretty, rose-scented cottage at Matfield, a village off the Tonbridge road in Kent.

Those were desperate days in England and particularly so in Kent. The Battle of Britain was under way. In one raid alone that afternoon, as Beveridge drove down to investigate murder at Crittenden, seventy German planes—Heinkels and Messerschmidts—had crossed the Straits of Dover. Vapour trails criss-crossed the blue skies. Bursts of machine-gun fire could be heard as our Spitfires and Hurricanes gave battle, and there was the continual crump of ack-ack fire. There was everywhere the sense that our destiny was being decided overhead.

To many people, maybe, murder on the ground might that day have seemed very smalltime. But not at the Yard. *Never* at the Yard, whatever battle is taking place elsewhere, for there is never a ceasefire between criminals and police.

Beveridge had a sharp eye for detail and a bold decisive mind. He looked like a policeman: tall and broad, soberly dressed in a dark suit and wearing the inevitable black 'Anthony Eden' hat so fashionable at the time. (*Every* man wore a hat in those days.) As he drove down to Matfield, Beveridge ran over in his mind the events that had led to his call from Scotland Yard.

Crittenden, the cottage he was heading for, was the home of Mrs. Dorothy Sanders Fisher, her daughter Freda, aged nineteen, and their middle-aged housekeeper Charlotte Saunders.

Mrs. Fisher's mother-in-law, old Mrs. Harriet Gibbs, who lives nearby, expected them to tea that day. In view of the aerial battles raging overhead she became frantic with worry when her repeated telephone calls to Crittenden went unanswered. So she sent her gardener to see what was wrong.

He found the bodies of all three women, clearly gunned down as they had run in terror through the orchard that screened Crittenden from the main Tonbridge road.

He found Freda Fisher first. She was lying across the orchard path, shot straight between the shoulder blades as she ran away. Then he found Mrs. Fisher. It looked as though she had seen the first killing and tried to make her getaway through knee-high grass and weeds. Then she had jumped over a ditch and got as far as a small wicker gate leading to the edge of a wood before the killer had caught up with her and shot *her* in the back, like her daughter.

The gardener went to the house. There was Miss Charlotte, the housekeeper, shot in turn as she came to the door to see what all the noise was about. The bullet had struck her between temple and ear.

There was a witness to the murders, but of no use to the police: a frightened whining dachshund that still ran frantically round the cottage.

Beveridge, the man with that radar eye for detail, checked all this over as he reached the cottage. He noted—how could he fail to note—all the obvious signs of breaking and entering. Clothing and papers strewn all over the floors. Desks and cupboards opened and emptied. He also saw, and this intrigued him much more, a woman's left-hand white hogskin glove lying roughly halfway between the two bodies of Mrs. Fisher and her daughter in the orchard. It was newish. It was not the sort of glove the Fishers would have worn for gardening. White, hogskin, very much out of place, one glove that might have been dropped, and a woman's glove: what was it doing there in the orchard of death?

Within minutes of his arrival, Peter Beveridge had the whole cottage under microscopic examination for fingerprints; a detailed search was under way of every locker, drawer, shelf, cupboard and basket for a companion to that curious and highly interesting white hogskin glove; and an inch-by-inch search was being made of the garden and orchard for possible murder weapon or cartridge cases.

Beveridge himself wandered round the cottage, room by room, looking for signs the murderer may have left behind.

That tray of broken crockery, for instance: Beveridge wanted to know more about that. Obviously it had been dropped on the stone floor when Miss Charlotte first heard the screams, or the shots, or both. Almost without thinking Beveridge began to put the pieces together. *Four* cups. *Four* saucers. The Fishers, who themselves were expected out to tea, must suddenly have told Miss Charlotte a guest would be calling on them. Who could it have been?

At this moment, Beveridge heard a positive report from one of his Murder Squad: no sign of a matching glove anywhere in the cottage, but plenty of money and a quite large amount of jewellery.

A sneakthief murder of three women by shooting never seemed less likely, and the Yard chief ordered full inquiries into the background of the women who had lived and died in the cottage.

Sir Bernard Spilsbury was already on his way down to conduct the post mortems. Inquiries with friends and relatives quickly established this picture of the Fishers' domestic life.

Just before the outbreak of the war, Mr. and Mrs. Walter Fisher had separated, apparently amicably enough. Each had a lover though neither sought a divorce. Eventually Mrs. Fisher, her daughter Freda, and Miss Charlotte the housekeeper settled at the Matfield cottage. Mr. Fisher retired to a farm at Piddington, near Bicester, in Oxfordshire which was owned by his mistress, a young widow named Mrs. Florence Iris Ouida ('Julia') Ransome.

Mrs. Ransome in fact now called herself 'Mrs. Fisher'. And there was one curious aside: she had brought in her mother and brother, a Mrs. Guilford and Fred Guilford, on to the farm to help run it without telling Mr. Fisher they were her relatives. Mrs. Ransome was slim, auburn-haired, and thirty-five years old. Peter Beveridge decided to call at her Piddington farm, seventy miles away, and drove there that night.

Like everyone else on the farm, she was asked to account

for her movements that day. She said she had not left the
farm. 'Ask the woman servant [Mrs. Guilford], she will tell
you the same,' said Mrs. Ransome. She admitted she knew
Mrs. Fisher and her daughter well and had often called on
them in the past.

The white hogskin glove was burning a hole in Beveridge's
pocket as he questioned Mrs. Ransome. As he left, he said
casually, 'By the way, would you mind trying this on?' and
pulled it from his coat pocket, holding it out to her.

'Certainly,' she said, 'although I think it is too small for
me.' Beveridge thought it fitted perfectly. He decided to
question Mrs. Guilford and quickly discovered she was in
fact Mrs. Ransome's mother. Nor was she entirely certain her
daughter had been home all day.

The Yard team motored back to Matfield. There Spilsbury told them: 'All three died from gunshot wounds.' No
cartridge cases had been found in the orchard but Beveridge,
with that sharp eye of his, had noted a .410 single-barrelled
shotgun at the Piddington farm a little earlier.

There were plenty of grounds for suspicion, but still precious
little tangible evidence to justify the arrest of Mrs. Ransome.
Beveridge sent his team out to conduct a house-to-house inquiry and find out if anyone had *seen* her at Crittenden that
afternoon.

Within twenty-four hours they traced thirteen people who
had seen—in the neighbourhood and at the critical time—a
woman wearing blue slacks and carrying a long, narrow,
brown paper parcel. There was the railway porter who saw
her get off the midday train at Tonbridge station (seven miles
away); a butcher's boy who saw her looking through the hedge
at the cottage; and a lorry driver who gave her a lift back to
Tonbridge railway station the same afternoon.

It was discovered Mrs. Ransome *had* borrowed the shotgun
and asked: 'How does it work? Will you show me how to
shoot rabbits with it?' It was also discovered that, a week
before the triple killing, Mrs. Ransome had asked how she

could learn to ride a bicycle. She had tried for a while and 'not done very well'.

After the killing, detectives had found Mrs. Fisher's bike abandoned in a ditch. The only fingerprints on it were the owner's: no clue there. But the detectives had wondered if the killer had tried to get away on it, had given up for some reason and dumped it in the ditch.

Mrs. Ransome had tried to do just that. Maybe, with her lack of experience—and burdened with the gun—she had given up after falling off too many times. And then sought a lift with the lorry driver. A return call at the Piddington farm showed Mrs. Ransome had gone to London, ostensibly to see her doctor.

Chief Superintendent Beveridge went back to London to arrest her. I went too, to cover the arrest. One of my contacts rang me and said he believed Mrs. Ransome was due to arrive at Waterloo station to meet a friend, and gave me the time of the train.

Stanley Sherman, a brilliant *Daily Express* photographer, was assigned to the story. We went to an office facing the station, gave our telephone number to my switchboard 'in case of emergency' and there Sherman set up a Long Tom camera capable of giving us a close-up shot of any arrest or scene that might develop.

The time passed the hour for the train arrival. Nothing. Sherman sat with his eyes glued to the station exits. He was chain-smoking and jumpy as a cat on hot bricks. Still nothing and we were beginning to lose hope when the 'phone rang.

'The rendezvous is changed,' said my informant. 'She is making for Holborn.' We left the Long Tom and all the expensive, heavy equipment, ran downstairs and hailed a taxi.

At the exact moment that our cab drew up in High Holborn, we saw Peter Beveridge standing in the doorway of David Samuels & Sons, printers and stationers. He was politely raising his Anthony Eden to a woman and saying, 'Mrs. Ransome, I believe? I hereby. . . .'

Sherman took the picture, from the taxi. It remains a classic crime picture, the detective towering above the slim woman at the moment he charged her with triple murder, the passers-by in the street wholly unaware of the drama being played out right beside them.

Her trial, which was postponed so that she could be kept under close medical watch, began on 8 November at the Old Bailey before Mr. Justice Tucker. The three-day trial, like the day of the triple murders, was held against a background of air raid warnings and hasty dashes to the air raid shelters. Mrs. Ransome was found guilty and sentenced to death. She was in the death cell and awaiting execution when she was certified insane and sent 'during His Majesty's pleasure' to Broadmoor.

Eight years later I read about her again in the *Evening Standard* (4 March, 1948). The article was headed: 'Broadmoor puts on a play.' The play was called *The Earl and the Girl.* All the actors and actresses were inmates of the world's most famous criminal lunatic asylum.

The last paragraph read:

'One of the most outstanding performances of the night was given by Daphne Brent. She played the part of a fairground dog trainer's girl friend and did so with an aplomb that would have startled many experienced actors and actresses.'

Daphne Brent was Mrs. Florence Iris Ouida ('Julia') Ransome, who killed three women in a mad fit of jealousy on a wartime summer's afternoon. And who was betrayed by a shattered teacup and a forgotten white hogskin glove.

# 7   Sherlock Holmes of the Yard

I am nearing my half-century as a crime reporter, and during that time it has been my privilege to meet the world's top detectives, on and off duty. Men like the late J. Edgar Hoover of the F.B.I., the heads of the Deuxième Bureau of France, and the Mounties: the faceless men who fight against atom spies, and others whose job it is to seize narcotics smuggled from the East into Europe and America.

But my second home has always been Scotland Yard. The best that the Yard has produced have no superior, to my mind, in any police force anywhere in the world. And if I had to go on the stand and swear to the one period in their long history that surpassed all others for successes scored against all the odds, I would refer to World War 2, especially during the Blitz.

It is hard for any young person today, the young policeman included, to imagine the difficulties facing the Yard chiefs of that time.

Manpower was desperately short; so was money. Every penny that in normal times would have been voted to Britain's crime-fighters (and it is never enough) was needed for the war against Hitler. The bombers came over every night, London burned as it had not done since the Great Fire, and it took the wisdom of a Solomon to say if the bodies found in the rubble might have died from enemy action or a common criminal's hand.

Newspapers were pitifully small in size. Crime coverage, so essential to every police force to spread the news into every house in the land—in the hope some vital witness can be alerted to come forward—was at a minimum.

Above all, there was the human factor. Policemen are no different from the rest of us. With a cluster of incendiaries or a string of high explosive bombs falling in streets where they had to trace and interview suspects, or merely seek witnesses who might not even want to help, any detective could be excused for taking the line of least resistance. Never could any Murder Squad have had a harder time.

Against this background, then, I rate Deputy Commander Bill Rawlings of Scotland Yard especially high on any list of great detectives. Rawlings could have been a successful barrister (he passed his Bar exams), but chose to solve crimes rather than prosecute criminals.

Physically, he came as near as any man to the image of Sherlock Holmes, Conan Doyle's super-detective from Baker Street. He was lofty; he walked with authority; he had a sharp intelligence; he had the same leanness of cheeks below a longish inquisitive nose. When he hit on a vital clue or listened to some promising new twist in a case, Rawlings' eyes would light up. He also had a reservoir of patience and doggedness that was marvellous to behold.

To my mind, Bill Rawlings never did a better job than solving the Dobkin Case.

I have no doubt at all there are many people walking freely in our midst who have got away with the perfect murder. Some years ago, I defined such a murder in my newspaper, the *Daily Express,* as: 'One in which the victim's body has passed beyond recovery—by cremation—and two well-intentioned, unsuspecting doctors have written the words "natural causes" across the death certificate.' Harry Dobkin lacked the cunning to plan a perfect murder, but he used the London Blitz as a cover for his crime—and he very nearly got clean away with it.

Hitler's Luftwaffe had taken such a mauling during the Battle of Britain, and the night-time terror Blitz that followed, that the citizens of London won a temporary respite in the middle of 1942.

On the morning of 17 July, workmen and air raid wardens were clearing the rubble from a wrecked Baptist Chapel in the Kennington Lane district of south-east London. Every workman clearing bomb debris anywhere in any city in Britain in those days was liable to come across a body. Routine instructions were in force everywhere. The foreman had to ring the police ('Another one!' they would say), the body was removed to the public mortuary and there medically examined. This was a police precaution, just to make quite sure the murderer *was* Adolf Hitler.

In the Baptist Chapel, a workman levered up a heavy stone slab apparently hurled from the churchyard in the blast of an explosion. Underneath he found a badly scorched skeleton. Parts of the arms and legs were missing, the skull was loosed from the body and the neck was bent forward below it. An everyday sight to the ARP workers: just another Blitz victim smothered in rubble, they thought.

Dr. Keith Simpson, pathologist, a household name today and for long a friend of mine, made the examination. Time of death: about twelve to eighteen months before. The body was of a woman aged between forty and fifty; approximately five feet in height, hair dark brown, turning grey (this from the few strands left). Lower jaw missing; upper jaw intact, signs she had worn a dental plate, with maybe seven false teeth.

Something about the way in which that neck was thrust forward suggested that the unknown woman may have tried to rise before being killed. That, and the sixth sense that always guides the good pathologist, decided Keith Simpson to probe a little deeper. He took another look at the bombed site. He found an unusual quantity of lime in the soil. Back in his laboratory in Guy's Hospital, Dr. Simpson took another look at the burned skeleton.

Next he found a tiny bone in the voice-box fractured. Many a killer has gone to the hangman because of a similar find. By itself, it is regarded as almost certain evidence of strangulation. In normal cases the pathologist can confirm such evidence by examining the victim's heart and lungs to prove asphyxia: here he could not. Nevertheless Dr. Keith Simpson felt sure he was dealing here not with a Blitz victim but someone who had been murdered by strangulation.

Enter Bill Rawlings of Scotland Yard.

I have said he looked like Sherlock Holmes—and in this case he needed all the great fictional character's qualities to help solve the case. He had to say to his team, 'We are trying to identify, in wartime London with its thousands of bombsites still uncleared, and its huge shifting population, one woman. Name unknown. Only a burned skeleton found. Dead, maybe twelve to eighteen months: aged forty to fifty, 5ft. tall or fractionally more, hair dark brown turning grey. *Your best bet*: that dental plate. Fillings found in four remaining teeth. Nothing more known.'

In the Missing Person's Register there were *at least* one thousand women who might answer to some parts of that meagre description. It required a huge process of elimination to leave those. So many relatives were seen; so many questions asked, in so many towns.

When did you last see your wife/mother/sister/girl-friend/cousin? Did she wear a dental plate in the upper jaw? What was the name of her dentist? Thank you sir/madam: we'll let you know as soon as we hear anything definite.

You can break the heart of a peacetime CID squad with a monumental task like that. It defies the imagination during a world war.

Finally they interviewed the sister of a woman named Mrs. Rachel Dobkin. She lived apart from her husband, said the sister, and had vanished on Good Friday 1941. Aged forty-one; height and hair colouring tallied. She had married Harry Dobkin in September 1920 and left him soon afterwards. She always had trouble in getting him to pay maintenance—at first anyway. Inquiries showed he had been meticulous in keeping them up since Easter 1941.

Intensive new inquiries led them to a Mr. Barnet Kopkin, a dentist in north London. He had treated Mrs. Dobkin for six years and had her dental charts. A replica of the plate he had made for Mrs. Dobkin fitted the jaw found in the Baptist Chapel.

Rawlings learned something else. The day after Mrs. Dobkin disappeared, a handbag containing her ration book and identity card—both absolutely vital in wartime—had been found in Guildford post office and had never been claimed. Maybe she had taken them there, but she had certainly come back to London to die. Perhaps the murderer had taken them there, and left them, to lay a false trail.

Before trying to find the husband, Rawlings concentrated his search instead on the immediate vicinity of the Kennington chapel. They found an ARP warden who remembered a fire in the chapel on the night of 15 April, 1941. Fires were their business: such dates were noted and remembered. Oddly enough there was no air-raid that night, but someone had reported seeing smoke coming through the floorboards of a school next to the chapel. The local police had called up the Fire Brigade.

After the flames had been put out, a London bobby—just standing by—had spotted a man hanging around and asked him who he was. 'I'm the firewatcher over there,' he answered, pointing to a block of offices nearby. And he made a curious, half-jocular remark which the bobby remembered: *'I didn't do it,'* he said.

The minister of the chapel also remembered something odd about the fire. Next day, when he went to look at his chapel, he found the remains of a partly burned straw mattress in the cellar. He had no idea how it had got there.

Rawlings told his men: 'Trace the firewatcher.' They reported back that he had since left, they were now looking for him, and they had a name: *Harry Dobkin.* He was brought in and questioned.

Mr. Dobkin was frank and open about the domestic situation. They had been living apart. She had always sought a reconciliation. He had as consistently refused.

'I last saw her on Good Friday last year [1941],' he said. 'We went to a café. She said, "If you don't make peace with me, I'll make trouble for you." But she has not tried to get in touch with me since.'

Another CID man in the Murder Squad, Detective Inspector Hatton, questioned Dobkin again. 'In fairness,' he warned Dobkin, 'I should tell you that human remains were found in the cellar of the chapel near where you were firewatching last April, and we are satisfied that they are those of your wife.'

Dobkin said: 'I don't know what you are talking about! I don't know of any cellar at the chapel, and I have never been down one there. In fact I don't believe it is my wife, but if you tell me it is so, I suppose I must accept it.'

Would he like to make a statement?

He would.

As he wrote, he did everything but put the hangman's rope round his neck. For he started off with these words: 'In respect to what you say that my wife has been found dead *or murdered. . . .*' No-one had mentioned the word 'murder'. Until that slip of the pen, Dobkin had merely been asked about a body found in a blitzed chapel cellar.

He was charged with the murder of his wife (still protesting his innocence). The evidence against him was overwhelming: the jury found him guilty after an absence of only twenty minutes. He was told in the death cell that a reprieve had been refused. Then he made a full confession.

The murder that turned out to be almost perfect—but for the intervention of Dr. Simpson and Deputy Commander William Rawlings, the Sherlock Holmes of the Yard—was in fact a very sordid little killing.

Mrs. Dobkin just wanted more money: Harry Dobkin was

too mean to part with any. So he killed her, staged the murder to look like one more death in the Blitz, and planted the handbag at Guildford to take inquiries away from London.

He was hanged on 27 January, 1943, at Wandsworth Jail.

In his deathcell confession, Dobkin told one wry joke against himself. At his trial great play was made of the fact that, while he had always dodged maintenance payments before Easter 1941, he had always paid promptly thereafter. Of course the payments were never collected, and Dobkin told of his huge embarrassment as he went each Monday to the local police station to pay his dues and was met with the unchanging wisecrack: 'Now, Harry, you know you've killed your old woman. What have you done with the body?'

If only they knew, thought Dobkin. If only they knew.

One thing is sure. Dobkin was mean and always hated to part with his money. But the payment he made every Monday, once the joke started, was far greater than anyone realised.

E

# 8   Charlie Artful

The wiliest bird I ever knew to fly high in the ranks of the Murder Squad was Jack Capstick. In private life Mr. Capstick delighted in growing roses and playing bowls. See him stroll down the road, with a magnificent bloom in his buttonhole, puffing contentedly at his pipe, with his grey hair neatly combed and his slightly tubby-hubby waistline, and he was everyone's typical next-door neighbour.

In his official capacity Detective Chief Superintendent John Capstick was a man to marvel at. He had the patience of Job. He was past master at moving into the very mind of an opponent and then, with deadly skill, analysing how best to outwit him.

He would adapt methods to cases with the natural ease and agility of a chameleon changing colour. He was gifted in a rare way: expert in all the tricks of the trade, quickwitted, wily and crafty as they came, a match for the slipperiest of customers who came into his orbit. Everyone, in the Yard itself, the underworld, and the Press, knew him as 'Charlie Artful'. He revelled in the tag. He was an artist, a supremely good catcher of criminals.

Charlie Artful had a brilliant record in the Murder Squad. All his cases were 'good', in the technical sense of tracking and trapping the quarry, so much so you could write a book about the man himself. But the one I think shows all his great qualities as a detective was the Harries double-murder in Carmarthen.

On 16 October, 1953, farmer John Harries and his wife Phoebe—a decent and highly respected old couple—vanished without trace from their holding at Derlwyn, near the village of Llanginning.

They disappeared after attending a Harvest Thanksgiving service at the local chapel on a Sunday evening. Just like that. In London and the big cities a couple can vanish, maybe, and weeks will go by before neighbours, who are brought up not to 'interfere', will raise the alarm. But not in the Welsh countryside, where the community is so tightly knit. I know Wales a little, and I know my Carmarthen. Here is some of the loveliest scenery in the whole country. Woods and green hills, and tumbling rivers: they still fish for salmon from the coracle—a wicker-built beetle craft that men carry on their backs exactly as the Ancient Britons did—right under the bridge in Carmarthen Town.

If it looks a little wild to the city visitor, a little spread out and rural, do not be fooled. Everyone has a job in the community and everyone knows everyone else. It is essentially a friendly community, and here is the big difference to the towns where it is considered 'interfering' to get too close to one's neighbours: in Carmarthenshire that friendliness gives a man the right to keep an eye on those around and ensure all is well.

It therefore followed, as surely as night follows day, that the disappearing of John and Phoebe Harries would be quickly noticed and talked about.

Only one person seemed to know that they had gone and where: their dark-eyed, handsome young nephew, Ronnie. He was the son of a butcher (another respected local man) and was married with one young child. Ronnie maintained to all who asked, including the local police, that his uncle and aunt had caught the train to London and gone off for a secret holiday. No-one else, it seemed, had seen them go or heard their plans.

They looked in at Derlwyn farm and found things that did

not match the story of a careful, elderly couple going on holiday. A joint ready for cooking, left in the oven to go bad: Mrs. Harries would never have done that voluntarily. Puzzlement turned into alarm; alarm into rumour; rumour into suspicion; and all into wild gossip that swept through that tightly-knit community of Jones the Post, Thomas the Bush (the name of a local hotel) and Evans the Bread, like wildfire.

Scotland Yard was called in to help solve the mystery. It is never easy for a stranger, particularly an official from London, to move in to a community like that and win the respect and affection he must have from the locals to solve such a case.

Charlie Artful, alias Det. Chief Superintendent John Capstick, was the man chosen. The new title the Welsh people gave him some weeks later, when he had found the missing couple—dead, alas—and charged one of their own with murder was proof in itself of his success: 'Capstick Whitehall'. It showed their respect for the Yard as well as the man, and Capstick was immensely proud to be known by those two names 'Capstick Whitehall' throughout Wales.

He stayed at an hotel in Carmarthen. So, of course, did his sergeant, Bill Heddon—a man with full legal training and a former lieutenant-colonel of Military Police. Almost every other room in that hotel was taken by reporters and photographers. Capstick got on well with the Press, he always did: but there were times when he had to move in secret. So at night when they worked (most nights!) the two Yard men would pointedly put their shoes outside the door for cleaning —the universal hotel sign for turning in—and then slip quietly out of the window and into a waiting police car to get away unobserved.

Like many a detective before him, Capstick had little doubt who his suspect was. He even had a motive—simple greed. But where were the bodies to be found in all that wild green countryside?

Ronnie Harries, of course, was prime suspect. For a time Capstick thought others—at least one other—might be involved, but after careful checking he ruled this out. Ronnie Harries was the last person to have 'seen' them go off on that secret holiday—the only one in fact. There was no proof they ever bought tickets and no sign they had ever arrived in London. There was the uncooked joint left in the oven of a woman who was never wasteful.

There was also the cheque. From the bank manager Capstick received a cheque, made out by John Harries right enough and apparently for the sum of £909. It was payable to Ronnie's father, but Ronnie himself had signed for it (on behalf of his father), and someone—it could only have been Ronnie—had altered the original figure that was written, £9—0s—9d. It was a crude alteration, unmistakable.

And there was the business of the cattle. Cattle need milking and feeding. They represent wealth to the aspiring farmer. Capstick quickly discovered that Ronnie Harries had transferred the stock to his father's place, Cadno Farm, above Pendine. And Ronnie had made no secret of the fact that he wanted to be a farmer himself.

You didn't need to be the brilliant detective Capstick undoubtedly was to select young Ronnie Harries as number one suspect. Capstick himself told me later he would have been quite prepared to arrest him for murder, even if the bodies had not been found. But he was determined to find those two old people, if indeed they could be found. There were many reasons for this. First, the professional ones. He wanted to know how they died, when they died, where they were buried. If that should be on the suspect's home ground, that was that. If not there were clues, maybe, that would point straight to the killer.

There was also a streak of compassion in the Capstick make up that he rarely showed. He would laugh and joke and turn a broad shoulder on the unpleasant facts of life, but it was there: and he did not want those two old people to be left to rot in some unknown grave. It was just not in his character, so he pushed on.

He called up every available policeman and soldier to search the secret Pendine rocket site for a possible burial place. He called on every farmer (except the Harries themselves) for help to search every nook and cranny, every ditch and culvert, every field and wood, in the land for miles around Derlwyn.

And how they responded! They came on foot, on tractor, with horse and cart and motorcar to listen to his request (given in English and Welsh—in the Welsh tongue by a local superintendent). To a farmer, time means money more than to anyone else: sowing time, time they can never get back. But they gave it generously: they poured in to help 'Capstick Whitehall'.

That night Capstick told me quietly: 'What really worries me is the wild life.' He knew Ronnie Harries was a skilled butcher and feared he may have dismembered the bodies.

'If those bodies are dismembered and scattered in the countryside,' he said, 'we may never find them—even the bones. The foxes and the buzzards will see to that.'

Every search drew a blank. The one farm that had not been searched was Cadno.

Capstick decided to flush Ronnie out, to make *him* point the way to the bodies. He and Heddon bought reel upon reel of sea-green cotton thread. At nights they crept down to the farm and—moving silently—wound the thin strands waist high over each exit from the farm into the fields.

Then they went back to the road above the farm and revved up the engine of their police car, loud and long. They used to watch the lamp light up in Ronnie's bedroom, and wait for him to come out of the house. Long after he had gone back to bed they would trace the breaks in the cotton and it transpired he always went into one field of growing kale.

'That's where we'll find them,' said Capstick. With the help of the local police—who, like all the Carmarthen people, gave him one hundred per cent support—he organised a search party of expert countrymen. Policemen all, who could read the signs around them as clearly as contours on a map. They went through the kale field inch by inch. Harries watched from his bedroom window.

A police sergeant spotted one patch of kale a little yellower, a little less high, than its green surround. He pushed a search stick down through the soft earth. It met resistance. A shout went up to Capstick. There—right under his feet—lay the remains of poor John and Phoebe Harries.

Ronnie was charged with their murder.

He denied the charge. His trial, at Carmarthen Assizes, gripped the imagination of the Welsh. The court was jam-packed. Hundreds more gathered outside, waiting for news. On 16 March, 1954, Ronald Harries was found guilty of the murder of his uncle and aunt, still protesting his innocence.

'I was their favourite,' he said.

It was the first conviction for murder in that court for sixty-five years. One month later he was hanged at Swansea Jail.

Charlie Artful, who had turned into Capstick Whitehall for the long Welsh murder hunt, won nation-wide publicity and acclaim for the patience he showed in conducting it.

At the Yard, his colleagues paid their own tribute. Over his desk they set a carved wooden plaque. *Softly, softly, catchee monkey,* it said.

Detective Chief Superintendent John Capstick was tickled pink.

# 9   The Alibi

Under the British legal system, where all men are presumed innocent until proven guilty, the alibi is of supreme import- ance. It is for the police to sound it, to hold it up to the light of investigation and see if it contains any chinks or cracks, never for the suspect to make it stand up. It follows that interrogation of a suspect is therefore a main weapon in the CID armoury.

You will hear all sorts of stories of what goes on inside the police station to get confessions. The story of Hume him- self gives the lie to the rumours. The secret of Scotland Yard's long and proud sequence of successes in the war against crime *lies in its mastery of interrogation.*

How do they get them to talk, the murderers and master criminals, who know their best chance of evading justice lies in silence? How do they get others to change carefully rehear- sed explanations? The answer lies in the individual detective's skill as an interrogator. It is an enormously difficult quality to analyse, mainly because this is an instinctive gift which cannot be taught. You can pass on the tips—but you can never teach the original skill which must always be adapting to circum- stances.

Fundamentally, I suppose, it is based on psychological insight. Some politicians have it: so do witchdoctors. The best reporters have it: so do all the best con men. Yet the wisest man in the world can be completely deficient of the gift.

The illiterate gypsy who makes his living out of horse-trading is undoubtedly master of the art. He will read the lies as they appear in the face of the man he is talking to—and he doesn't need to look at his eyes. His ear is subtle enough to detect the slightest variation in tone, the slightest inflexion that tells him—as accurately as any lie detector—when the man sitting opposite is worried, and when he thinks he has nothing to hide.

All the pros at Scotland Yard have it. One of them told me, over drinks, how he had weighed up the art of interrogation. He said:

'Suppose you are interrogating the man: simply interrogating and not, for the moment, charging him. The approach, the first few sentences you utter, are vitally important. So I suggest something away from the vital subject if possible (it isn't always): some small talk about his personal or family life, or even about his job.

'Try to think what the other fellow is thinking. Surely, assuming him to be guilty—and if he isn't or you didn't think he might be, you wouldn't be questioning him anyway—his main interest at this moment will be to find out how much *you* know!

'It is therefore immensely important that you realise that your suspect will possibly try to reverse the roles: to take over himself the part of interrogator.

'All right. How much are you going to tell him? And when are you going to tell it? You must have the answers to these two questions quite clear in your mind before you walk in and begin with that apparently friendly approach—and before you offer him your cigarette case.

'Another thing. It is of fundamental importance that you should not only appear to be friendly, you must also be *fair*. If the suspect feels you are trying to trap him or force information out of him, he will be on his guard at once.

'The important thing is to get him talking. Once he begins he will do your work for you. Generally speaking it is bad psychology to shoot the vital questions at him too soon.

'If, as often happens, you have several hours ahead of you in a train or an airplane with a man who knows he is under suspicion, you can be quite sure he is only too eager to talk. This is partly because he wants desperately to find out how much *you* know. But also, I think, because towards the end, the criminal senses the weakness of his position and seeks human companionship, someone's shoulder to cry on, even with the man who has brought him to book. Never, never underestimate this fundamental need.

'The best way to utilise it always is to let him talk. Don't, therefore, appear to focus too much attention on what he is saying, on his admissions. Appear to listen casually, even with an attitude of indifference.

'When something incriminating is said, it is good tactics sometimes to show no particular interest, to leave the subject for a while, and returning to it later *as if it is accepted* that this is a matter on which the two of you share certain information.

'If you marshal your observations in the form of an argument, you are almost certain to appeal to the intelligent or educated suspect, who is sure to want to explain points you may not have appreciated, or perhaps to argue with you when he does not accept your conclusions. Fine! Let him run on.

'Ten to one you'll be wasting your time even trying that technique with an uneducated suspect. More than likely he will listen to you in silence—and do himself no harm whatever in the process. Always remember: horses for courses!

'Never forget how open to flattery most people are. *Nine times out of ten a man is the hero of his own stories.* Play gently on the weakness and you will be far better rewarded than if you adopt an aggressive attitude.'

With the murder suspect, an experienced detective knows that physical violence is strictly for the Gestapo. Maybe he has just seen the mutilated body of a child, and quite possibly he thinks a damned good hiding too light a punishment by far for the man responsible; but he knows, too, that the process is self-defeating.

Use the psychological approach. It is infinitely more rewarding. This is text-book instruction for the Murder Squad.

Take the case of Leslie Green, the twenty-nine-year-old murderer who thought he had an absolutely cast-iron, unbreakable alibi. He reckoned without the remarkable powers of Det. Superintendent Reg Spooner (as he then was) in the vital business of interrogation.

Spooner was a big man with the knack of looking not like a tough guy but always like a big St. Bernard dog: someone you could talk to and trust, for there was an air of reliability always about him. He was very shrewd, he was a most versatile policeman, and, in my opinion, had few equals in Murder Squad history. He had an eye for detail, patience aplenty, and was self-critical at all times. Above all, Spooner was fair.

Young Green sat at a table facing Spooner, and was clearly growing more confident with every passing minute of the interrogation. He felt sure there was no direct evidence against him.

He felt extremely confident about the questioning. This man Spooner was dead easy to talk to! He had seen right through him in the opening stages—always the trickiest part, so he had been told—and now, like a poker player who feels sure he has an unbeatable hand, he was just stringing Spooner along.

From time to time he dropped hints to show he had a first-class alibi. Suggestions made, not with the sudden afterthought of a worried-but-innocent man whose mind is jogged by a fragment of memory, nor with the assuredness of a calm and reasonable man who feels 'It's all a silly mistake which has *got* to be cleared up soon'.

No: Green was casually introducing a fact here, a fact there —like an actor with a throw-away line—but he clearly meant them all to register with Spooner. But Spooner knew all about the value of a poker face himself. He had used his in wartime

service (with M.I.5)—in duels with the spies he had interro-
gated and with the traitor atom-scientists he had questioned
afterwards.

Right now, Spooner sat there opposite Green, shoulders
drooped, the perpetual cigarette stuck to his lip, face expres-
sionless, listening to the suspect talk. Patiently, missing
nothing, the Murder Squad man was sifting every word of
the carefully planted alibi, running it through in his mind.

Spooner and Det. Sgt. Ernest Millen, another brilliant
policeman, destined to become head of the C.I.D. at the Yard,
had gone to Staffordshire ten days earlier after the body of
sixty-two-year-old Mrs. Alice Wiltshaw had been found in
her fourteen-roomed home at Barlaston. It was 1952. She
had been beaten to death.

The weapon, a heavy, old-fashioned poker, was found in
the kitchen. Ransacked dressing tables in the bedrooms told
a silent story of the £5,000 worth of jewellery that had been
stolen. On his way out, the killer had stopped to wrench
another two rings from his victim's fingers.

A typical case of murder for greed. At first sight, the work
of anyone who happened to be passing: any stranger. Spooner
himself had weighed this theory and mentally rejected it for
the following reasons:

The thief and murderer had entered the house by way of
an overgrown spinney path: hard to spot, unlikely to be
used by a total stranger. There were easier ways available.

The only rooms in the big house that had been disturbed
were the ones in which Mrs. Wiltshaw kept her jewels. No
need to 'case the joint': here was someone who appeared to
know his way around from the moment he broke in.

And there was the time factor. The killer had broken in at
around five-thirty in the evening. It was dangerously close to
the time when Mr. Wiltshaw arrived home. Professional jewel
thieves on this type of job spend their time watching, noting,
timing the moves of everyone in the house. They would be
likely to avoid the chance of meeting up with the husband.

Perhaps this was someone who had everything timed to fit in
—with a carefully prepared alibi.

Mr. Wiltshaw, in fact, returned home within fifteen minutes
of his wife's murder. To Spooner, everything pointed to a
killer who knew the house and the household routine. His
obvious and clear next step in the murder investigation was
to question every suspect that theory involved: relatives,
friends, neighbours, tradesmen and servants. All the rest, the
professional jewel thieves, convicts at large, local thugs,
Spooner left for the moment to one side.

Now, at this table, Spooner had come to the last name on
the long list of people who came under this heading. The man
he was talking to, Leslie Green, was former chauffeur-gardener
to the Wiltshaws. Like all the others Green seemed at first
sight 'in the clear'. All those carefully dropped fragments of
information in his talk with Spooner underlined the alibi, that
he was twelve miles away at the moment Mrs. Wiltshaw was
bludgeoned to death.

Spooner took another long look at his man. His eyes travelled down to the shoes. They were rubber soled and foreign
looking. Now whoever had committed murder there had left
one footprint on the highly polished kitchen floor of the man-
sion: made by a rubber-soled shoe of similar size. There was
one discrepancy. The footprint left behind had a clear mark,
a crease, right across the sole. Green's shoe had no such mark.
Still, it fitted for size. Spooner decided to ask a few background
questions into the movement of this confident, assured man.

Millen and his Murder Squad team started digging. They
found Green was living well above his income. He was married, with a wife and child to provide for: he also had a
'fiancée'—a nurse in Leeds.

On the eve of his 'engagement' Green had shown the girl
(an innocent party) two rings. Friends said their description
was identical with the two torn from the dead woman's hand.
Circumstantial evidence but not direct.

And Leslie Green, *using the name of Wiltshaw*, stayed at

the Metropole Hotel, Leeds, on the night before the murder. Interesting, but still not direct evidence.

Two days after the murder, Green told another nurse at the hospital his 'aunt', Mrs. Wiltshaw, had been attacked with an old-fashioned heavy poker. Spooner had deliberately not mentioned the weapon used. Most interesting—but still no direct evidence.

Now Spooner took a closer look at Green's alibi. A number of people at the Station Hotel in Stafford—with whom Green had been associating on the day of the killing—were questioned, and there was a clear interval of time when Green was out of their sight. A train left Stafford at 5.10 p.m. to reach Barlaston at 5.35. There was a train back, arriving at Stafford at 6.26 p.m.—leaving an interval of half an hour, ample time for murder and robbery. No one had seen Green in this period.

The hotel manager himself, a former RAF man, happened to notice that when Green left later, to catch the 7.58 p.m. train to Leeds, he was carrying a Royal Air Force macintosh. A similar coat was missing from the Wiltshaw home. Spooner ordered a check on all railway lost property offices. The macintosh was traced—handed in just after that 7.58 train drew in to Holyhead.

In Leslie Green's pockets there was a letter mentioning an address in Belmont Grove, Leeds. 'Search that house,' said Spooner. 'From top to bottom.'

The police did just that—and it cost them £50 later to make good the damage. They even pulled up the floorboards. There they found the two missing rings, but to this day the rest of the jewellery has not been found.

Now Spooner saw Green again and this time told him to try on a bloodstained left-hand glove picked up by the Murder Squad searchers in a ditch at Barlaston. It fitted. The thumb of the glove was cut through, and Green's thumb bore a scar at this identical spot.

It left him with the question of the footprint with a line running across the sole. The lab technicians told him that if the man was moving, then the print could have borne such a crease.

'Of course he was moving!' said Spooner. 'He was murdering Mrs. Wiltshaw at that moment.'

Green was charged and sent for trial. He 'did a Hume' and invented two burglars who, he swore, had handed him the incriminating rings at eleven o'clock on the morning of 17 July. Spooner knew, and so told the jury, this was *ten hours after* he had shown them to the nurse in Leeds. The alibi was blown skyhigh.

Leslie Green was sentenced to death and executed on 23 December, 1952.

At the trial, Green told his warders: 'If Spooner gets me hanged, I'll come back and haunt him.' By an astonishing coincidence, Spooner had come to terms with this spooky possibility a year before.

Donald Seaman, a colleague of mine on the *Daily Express*, had given evidence in 1951 at the murder trial of Herbert Leonard Mills. His evidence was damning and Mills—a crippled teenager—was duly hanged. Supt. Spooner was the man at Scotland Yard who had taken Seaman's statement. Three months after the hanging, Seaman went back to Spooner and said: 'I can't sleep at nights. Every time I shut my eyes I see a picture of this kid. *It haunts me* and I just don't know what to do. You have sent so many murderers to the scaffold. Can you help me?'

Spooner could and he did. He pointed out that the law of the country demanded an eye for an eye and a tooth for a tooth. 'Mills was properly convicted,' he said. 'If he had got away with this murder he might have tried again and it could have been one of your family next time. Don't fool yourself: I never do. Society is better off without such people. Every detective in the world has to believe that or his job would become intolerable.'

Seaman was never haunted again. And Spooner remained singularly unmoved by Green's threat. After the hanging, and until the day of his death (Spooner died of cancer before his retirement) he confided to me that insomnia was the least of his problems.

I mourn Spooner, who was a brilliant detective and a superb psychologist. Spooner and Millen: there was a team the Murder Squad will be lucky to equal, never mind excel.

# 10  The Acid Bath Killer

The mind of a murderer is uncharted territory to most normal folk. Consider the triple murders committed by Michael Bassett, of Barlaston, in Staffordshire. He shot two pretty young French sisters, Claudine and Monique Liebert and their twenty-year-old boyfriend, Daniel Berland, to death as they toured Britain on a camping holiday in July 1971.

He was twenty-five years old. Before he committed suicide, by gassing himself in his car, he wrote this letter to say why he took three innocent lives:

'To whom it may concern.

'To save a lot of police time and public money, I hereby confess to the murder of three persons camping at Mouldsworth.

'I shot them with a .22 automatic rifle, which I stole the day before from a fairground at Rhyl, together with three magazines and about 100 rounds of .22 short Remington cartridges.

'In all, I fired about 20 rounds at the three of them. They had provoked me, so I taught them a lesson.'

Before he left the death campsite, he carefully left a clue for the Murder Squad—his fingerprints on a cider flagon nearby.

Now why should he—how could *anyone*—behave like that? He wrote one explanation to his sister by adoption, saying 'I

F

feel . ₂ . the only way to get away from all my lies, sins, failures, and general uselessness is to turn myself off, as it were. When you are not happy with doing evil things, they escalate. One sin levels to a greater sin and finally to the ultimate sin.'

His letter to the police is concise and carefully worded. His letter to his adopted sister defies analysis. What doors opened and closed in his mind to urge his fingers to write both within hours of committing triple murder we shall never know.

Criminal history abounds with similar riddles, and studies of the mind of such killers abound with terms such as schizophrenia, hysteria, paranoia, epileptic, melancholic and so on. They point the way to an explanation, but no more. For instance, to this day no-one knows why Peter Kurten, 'The Monster of Dusseldorf', committed nine murders, including five children, during the winter of 1929. Once arrested, he said that he felt compelled to strike at weekly and even daily intervals. The doctors who examined him listed sexual mania, pyromania (he admitted forty cases of arson too) and delusions of grandeur in his mental makeup. But was he mad or just downright bad?

Then there are aggressive psychopaths, like Michael Bassett. He reacted violently to some minor situation which arose with those three campers—my guess is that they laughed at him and told him to 'buzz off'. These psychopaths are, to use the expression of a famous forensic specialist, 'not sane enough to be at large, but mad enough to be in Bedlam'.

Such a man, too, was young Miles Gifford who murdered both his parents in 1954 by hitting them over the head and hurling their bodies over a Cornish cliff. After the murders, Gifford pawned his mother's jewellery and spent the proceeds on a night out with a girl. During the evening's 'entertainment' he confessed to the killings!

Thirteen years before, a psychiatrist had warned Gifford's mother and father that 'the door is slowly closing on your boy's sanity'. At his trial, experts attributed this same boy's schizophrenia to 'a sadistic nanny who had repeatedly locked him during infancy in a dark cupboard'.

Mad enough to be in Bedlam? Or wholly bad? The jury found him guilty, not insane, and he was duly hanged.

Christie—John Reginald Halliday Christie, the necrophiliac strangler of 10 Rillington Place—was labelled an hysteric by one scientific witness at his trial: meaning victim of an illness which results in the splitting of personality in its severest form. Christie murdered six women, including his wife, and made love to them after death. Professor Francis Camps propounded the theory that Christie had reached a stage of sexual incapability and the woman needed to be unconscious before he could possess her.

Incidentally he was a chronic hypochondriac, forever wallowing in past illnesses, real or imaginary. He lost his voice for a period of three-and-a-half years after a wartime air raid in which he claimed to have been blown up. True or not, the loss of voice was the psychological effect of hysteria: there was no physical cause. And he regained the full power of speech at moments of emotional stress.

At his trial the experts said his state of mind following the death of his wife was 'completely vague', that he killed compulsively—and would have continued if he had not been caught—because it was the only way of satisfying this frustrated sex impulse.

Frustrated? Mad? Or a repellent pervert who went on the run in London once he was found out? Too late to argue now, for Christie was hanged.

And there was Haigh, the acid bath killer. During and after his trial the wrangling went on—was he mad or was he faking insanity?

The editorial column of the *Medico-Legal Journal* of 1950 had this to say:

'The "perfect crime" is a novelist's dream, and yet, from time to time, a diabolically inspired criminal has all but succeeded in achieving this end.

'It was Crippen's subsequent indiscretion and precipitancy in attempting to escape with his paramour which aroused the further suspicions of the authorities, and so led to the discovery of the only remaining identifiable fragment of the integument [external skin] of the late Mrs. Crippen.

'Ruxton drew to the full on his special medical knowledge, but nonetheless patient reconstruction with such fragments as remained, defeated his attempt to destroy all traces of the identity of his victims.

'Dr. Keith Simpson recently honoured the Society with an account of the Haigh "Acid Bath Murder", and we publish his paper and the subsequent discussion elsewhere.

'It was revealed by one of the police officers concerned in the preliminary investigations that, but for Haigh's arrogant assurance that he had completely destroyed all trace of the late Mrs. Durand-Deacon, *he might not have been convicted.*

'The acid sludge which contained the sole fragments remaining of that unfortunate lady and her personal possessions, was still actively working when Haigh let slip this—for him—unfortunate remark.

'Further delay would have led to the total destruction of all trace of the dead woman.

'All of which,' concluded the *Medico-Legal Journal* of the day, 'goes to show that however scientifically clever the criminal may be, it is the human weaknesses that may lead to his undoing.

'The police inquisitor must be eternally on the *qui vive* for this chink in the armour, and it may well be that until he has discovered it, all the impressive array of scientific investigation is . . . kept at bay.'

All very fine and dandy. I agree with most of it. But it pre-supposes that each murder investigation depends on the final interrogation, with the killer happily making some mistake and the detective spotting it at once. There is a lot more to it than that.

Every member of a Murder Squad, and for practical purposes that extends from those specialists inside the Yard right down to each policeman or woman who makes the very first inquiry in the case, must possess that most sensitive item of all police equipment—*intuition*.

The good cop, man or woman, has a nose for the unusual, the not-quite-right circumstance. They will come away from that preliminary inquiry with a distinct feeling of unease: they communicate it to their superior officer whose own antennae feel out over the facts and begin to worry and wonder. If the nose *has* detected the smell of foul play and the original reaction is right, you will have a lead that will guide all the following impressive array of scientific investigation.

As in the case of Woman Police Sergeant Alexandra Maud Lambourne, from the Chelsea police division, when she first met John George Haigh.

She was making a routine 'missing persons' inquiry. When any person is reported missing, the details are relayed to all Metropolitan police stations by teleprinter. They are also published in the current edition of the *Police Gazette* and circulated in that way to every station house in the country.

Sergeant Lambourne was making her missing persons call in 1949. In that year no less than 1,241 people vanished from their homes in Britain. They disappeared for a variety of reasons. Many were plain restless after the war; not a few fell in love, went off with the new partner, became disillusioned and came back; many slipped off to dodge debts; or theirs were petty quarrels. A score of reasons: but in those days of the identity card and ration book in postwar austerity Britain it was not easy to disappear by assuming a new identity, and most of the missing persons came back. At the end of that year, only twenty men and six women remained unaccounted for.

Sergeant Lambourne knew about these trends and all about human frailties—she was an excellent police officer—and while she was thorough, that first call was still routine.

Mrs. Olive Durand-Deacon, the woman reported missing, was aged sixty-nine, well-to-do, a sincere and gentle soul (she was an ardent Christian Scientist) and not the sort to wander off for any complicated reason. Most likely, with a woman of her age, it was a case of lost memory. It so often happened. She was living in a quiet and wholly respectable Kensington hotel. The cities of Britain are full of such hotels, and the hotels are full of clients similar to Mrs. Durand-Deacon.

Sergeant Lambourne spoke to all the staff and a number of the guests. Mrs. Constance Lane, a close friend of hers who also lived in the hotel and who actually initiated the inquiry, was the last person to see the missing woman. She had helped her on with her Persian lamb coat, she said, as they stood on the front steps of the hotel. She had asked casually, 'Are you going shopping?'

Mrs. Durand-Deacon answered: 'Oh no, I am going to Crawley with Mr. Haigh.' Crawley is now a New Town in Sussex. In those days there was only the old town: small, sleepy enough, only an hour's drive from London.

Mr. Haigh was a business man of nearly forty who stayed at the hotel and occasionally shared a dinner-table with the sixty-nine-year-old Mrs. Durand-Deacon. He told the woman police sergeant:

'She arranged to come down to Crawley to see my factory. She wanted to buy some samples of plastic finger-nails: I had invented a process and she thought they might be manufactured. We arranged that I should pick her up at the Army & Navy Stores and drive her down to the factory. But she never turned up, so I came back to the hotel.'

Sergeant Lambourne had no reason whatever at this stage to disbelieve Haigh or even question his story, but as she listened to him, she used her intuition (both as woman and police sergeant) and did not like what she found.

He was neat and clean and polite. He was also glib and, like Uriah Heep, kept washing his hands with invisible soap. She didn't like his eyes: they were small and shifty and kept darting about as he spoke. Sergeant Lambourne came to the definite conclusion during that brief interview that he was not the sort of man she would care to have sharing her dinner-table. With nothing more than that to go on, she went back to Chelsea police station and reported to Chief Inspector Shelley Symes.

'There's something about him,' she said, 'that doesn't *sound* right.' Symes did not hesitate. He put in a call to C.R.O. (the Criminal Records Office) and asked if anything was known about a John George Haigh.

There was. C.R.O. index card number 86522 listed a John George Haigh sentenced to four years at Surrey Assizes in November 1937 for obtaining money by false pretences and to a further twenty-one months at London Sessions, in June 1941, for theft.

Symes ordered routine police procedure for a watch on Haigh's movements, a request to the West Sussex police for a thorough search of the factory at Crawley, and a check with jewellers and pawnbrokers for any trace of the jewellery Mrs. Durand-Deacon was known to be wearing at the time of her disappearance.

The report from Crawley proved highly interesting. The police there found three carboys (glass bottles in frames) which had contained some form of acid, a rubber apron and gloves, a .38 revolver and eight rounds of ammunition, a cleaner's receipt for a Persian lamb coat and a leather case containing papers relating to a Dr. and Mrs. Rosalie Henderson and a family named McSwan.

Shelley Symes sent one of his men to Sussex to claim the coat from the cleaners. Haigh was escorted to Chelsea police station and at once admitted he had taken it to the cleaners. He said it belonged to a Mrs. Henderson and that he was managing her affairs while she was on holiday in South Africa.

The Chief Inspector went back to Mrs. Durand-Deacon's hotel and searched her apartment again. In a workbox he found some lining fabric which, to the naked eye, seemed to match lining recently repaired in the Persian lamb coat. He sent coat and fabric to the police laboratory for detailed comparison. Back came the report: the fabric found in the workbox and the pieces used to repair the Persian lamb coat came from an identical piece of cloth. The police scientists also found traces of human blood on the coat collar.

Another telephone call came in to the Chelsea CID room, this time from a jeweller in Horsham, near Crawley. He had bought jewellery similar to that worn by Mrs. Durand-Deacon from a man calling himself 'J. McLean' of St. George's Drive, London, S.W. And he was under the distinct impression he had bought more jewellery from the same man a year before, and on that occasion the man called himself 'J. G. Haigh'.

Symes called up his men who were tailing Haigh—and had been, ever since Sergeant Lambourne had reported her first intuitive suspicions—to say: 'Bring him in.'

One of the first things Haigh said after he reached Chelsea was: 'Tell me, frankly, what are the chances of anyone being released from Broadmoor?'

An inspector replied: 'I cannot discuss that sort of thing with you.'

From Haigh then came one of the most horrific murder stories heard anywhere in the world: of a human vampire at work, a killer who drank the blood of his victims.

This is *exactly* how it went.

HAIGH: 'Well, if I told you the truth, you would not believe me. It sounds too fantastic for belief.'

DET. INSPECTOR WEBB: 'I must caution you. . . .'

HAIGH: 'I understand all that. *Mrs. Durand-Deacon no longer exists!* She has disappeared completely and no trace of her can ever be found.'

WEBB: 'What has happened to her?'

HAIGH: 'I have destroyed her with acid. You will find the sludge that remains at Crawley. I did the same with the Hendersons and the McSwans. Every trace has gone. How can you prove murder if there is no body?'

Haigh sat there, looking at Webb, arrogantly calm and composed. He was being too clever by half, but neither of the two men knew it at the time. Inspector Webb called Detective Superintendant Tom Barratt (another fine murder investigator) and Shelley Symes into the room.

With the three policemen and Haigh was a shorthand writer. No leading questions were asked as Haigh 'spilled the beans'. They let him run on in a gruesome serial of murder confessions. He said: 'I have already made some statements to you about the disappearance of Mrs. Durand-Deacon. I have been worried about the matter and fenced about, in the hope you would not find out about it. The truth is, however, that we left the hotel together and went to Crawley in my car.

'She was inviegled into going to Crawley by me, in view of her interest in artificial finger-nails. Having taken her into the storeroom at Leopold Road, I shot her in the back of the head, whilst she was examining some paper for use as finger-nails.

'Then I went out to the car and fetched in a drinking glass and made an incision (I think with a penknife) in the side of the throat, and collected a glass of blood, which I then drank.

'Following that I removed the coat she was wearing, a Persian lamb, and the jewellery—rings, necklace, ear-rings and cruciform—and put her in a forty-five-gallon tank. I then filled the tank up with sulphuric acid, by means of a stirrup pump, from a carboy. I then left it to react.

'I should have said that in between putting her in the tank and pumping in the acid, I went round to the Ancient Priors for a cup of tea.

'Having left the tank to react, I brought the jewellery and revolver into the car, and left the coat on the bench. I went to the George [an hotel in Crawley] for dinner and I remember I was late, about ninish. I then came back to town and returned to the hotel at Kensington about 10.30.

'The following morning I had breakfast and discussed the disappearance of Mrs. Durand-Deacon with the waitress and Mrs. Lane.'

At this point Haigh, who had told of murder, drinking human blood, disposal of the body by acid and of taking tea and dinner with undiminished appetite—all virtually in the same breath—told how he got rid of Mrs. Durand-Deacon's belongings. Then he switched to the murders of his other known victims.

At all times Haigh was businesslike and direct, a ghoulish figure, never showing remorse or pity. Behind his words lay the unspoken taunt 'what good will they do you without the bodies?'

Haigh continued: 'The ration books and clothing coupon books and other documents in the names of McSwan and Henderson are the subject of another story.

'This is covered very briefly by the fact that in 1944 I disposed of William Donald McSwan in a similar manner to the above in the basement of 79 Gloucester Road, London S.W.7 and of Donald McSwan and Amy McSwan in 1946 at the same address, and in 1948 of Dr. Archibald Henderson and his wife Rosalie, also in a similar manner, at Leopold Road, Crawley.

'Going back to the McSwans, William Donald, the son, whose address at that particular time I can't remember, met me at The Goat public house in Kensington High Street, and from there we went to 79 Gloucester Road, where—in the basement which I had rented—I hit him on the head with a cosh, withdrew a glass of blood from his throat as before, and drank it. He was dead within five minutes or so.

'I put him in a forty-gallon tank and disposed of him with acid as in the case of Mrs. Durand-Deacon, disposing of the sludge down a manhole in the basement. I took his watch and odds and ends, including an identity card, before putting him in the tank.

'I had known this McSwan, and his mother and father, for some time and on seeing his mother and father explained that he had gone off to avoid Army call-up. I wrote a number of letters in due course purporting to come from him and posted in, I think, Glasgow and Edinburgh, explaining various details of the disposition of properties which were to follow.

'In the following year I took separately to the same basement the father Donald and the mother, Amy, disposing of them in exactly the same way as the son.

'The files of the McSwans are at my hotel and will give details of the properties which I disposed of after their deaths. I have since got additional ration books by producing their identity cards in the usual way.

'I met the Hendersons by answering an advertisement offering for sale their property at 22 Ladbroke Square. They sold it and moved to 16 Dawes Road, Fulham. This runs in a period from November 1947 to February 1948.

'In February 1948, the Hendersons were staying at Kingsgate Castle, Kent. I visited them there and went with them to Brighton, where they stayed at the Metropole. From here I took Dr. Henderson to Crawley and disposed of him by shooting him in the head with his own revolver, which I had taken with his property at Dawes Road. I put him in a tank of acid, as in the other cases. That was in the morning, and I went back to Brighton and brought up Mrs. Henderson on the pretext that her husband was ill. I shot her in the store room, and put her in another tank, and disposed of her with acid.

'In each of the last four cases,' said Haigh, 'I had my glass of blood as before.'

Then he went on in that businesslike way:

'In the case of Dr. Henderson, I removed his gold cigarette case, his gold pocket watch and chain, and from his wife her wedding ring and diamond ring, and disposed of all this to Bull's at Horsham for about £300. I paid their bill at the Hotel Metropole, collected their luggage and their red setter, and took the luggage to Dawes Road.

'The dog I kept for a period at the hotel, until I had to send him to Professor Sorsby's kennels in the country, on account of night blindness. By means of letters purporting to come from the Hendersons, I kept the relatives quiet, by sending the letters to Mrs. Henderson's brother Arnold Burlin, who lives in Manchester.'

Barratt, Symes and Webb were all experienced detectives and no strangers to murder. But they told me they walked out of that interview room 'like old men' and then worked out plans to obtain physical confirmation of Haigh's appalling claims.

For the crime reporters this was a tantalising case. We knew enough to sell newspapers by the million, but were prevented by the rules of contempt of court from printing what we knew. One newspaper, the *Daily Mirror*, ran a story about the Human Vampire: it was fined a huge sum and its editor sent to jail.

I went down to Crawley with Superintendent Guy Mahon of the Yard, Dr. Keith Simpson, the Home Office pathologist, and Dr. G. E. Turfitt, deputy director of the Metropolitan Police Laboratory. I watched as during the next few days 475 lbs. of dirty, greasy and partly charred muck was dug up and sent to London for analysis. It was searched by men who spread it out over a whole range of steel trays and put it, section by section, piece by filthy piece, onto the benches at the laboratory. No-one knew just what to expect.

From it all they recovered: three gall stones (of human type); part of someone's left foot; eighteen fragments of human bone, all eroded to some extent; full upper and lower dentures—intact and later positively identified as those supplied by a dentist to Mrs. Durand-Deacon; the handle of a red plastic handbag similar to the one she carried; and the cap of a lipstick holder.

A plastic cast made by Superintendent Cyril Cuthbert of the Yard laboratory of the foot showed some comparison between it and the left foot of the victim. Those indications of sex which remained pointed to female. The bone fragments left indicated someone in late adult age: Mrs. Durand-Deacon!

Haigh was hanged on 10 August, 1949.

Not for the first time in my career as an observer of human frailties, I thought death as prescribed by the State too merciful. I repeat that without equivocation. My job then was to record, not to judge. I have given Haigh's statement so fully now because I believe it to be of value although Parliament has voted that death by hanging is something that belongs to another, and less enlightened, age.

To go back for a moment to that editorial in the *Medico-Legal Journal*: of course, it was Haigh's boast that he had destroyed all trace of Mrs. Durand-Deacon that put him on the scaffold. The acid sludge was still at work. Days, weeks might have gone by before the police had examined that dreadful factory yard. The few remains that *were* found would have vanished completely. Even the dentures would have dissolved in another three weeks.

You will find many arguing still that Haigh was insane. He was certainly a man who put life on a lower plane than would you or I. He was quite indifferent to murder. But it has always been plain to me—by his actions—that he knew at all times what he was doing and that he took deliberate steps to avoid discovery.

The authorities took extreme steps to establish that Haigh was *not* insane in the eyes of the law. He was examined, over a lengthy period, by no less than twelve qualified medical men. Six were prison doctors, which means that, apart from normal medical qualifications, they had considerable experience of the criminal mind. All twelve were convinced Haigh was simulating insanity. Some of the tests included recordings made of his 'brainwaves' and his reactions to 'ink-blot' tests. The doctors believed Haigh over-played his 'mad' reactions.

I used a more simple test. I simply recalled his first question to Detective Inspector Webb: 'Tell me frankly, what are the chances of anyone being released from Broadmoor?'

Haigh was found to be a legally sane monster who killed for greed. It is a view with which I wholeheartedly agree. I do not say *normal*. No-one can be 'normal' and behave as he

did. The dividing line is defined in the McNaughten Rules,
thus: did he know at the time that what he was doing was
wrong?

It is only fair to record that his childhood was dreadful.
His family may have loved their choirboy son (it is said they
did), but they were religious fanatics, and his father went to
fantastic lengths to protect the family against sin. He built
a high wall round the garden 'to protect us from the evil
world'. He bore a cross-shaped scar on his forehead and told
his son, 'It is the brand of Satan'. In fact, it was the result
of a mine accident. If anyone was abnormal in that household, it was surely Haigh's father: a typical paranoid.

Maybe Haigh grew up believing he was the son of a sinner,
and therefore doomed himself. There is some evidence to support the 'hidden guilt' complex. The way he dry-washed and
wet-washed his hands, both in conversation and under the tap.
He even wore gloves in mid-summer to keep his hands clean!

I daresay it can be interpreted as a *Macbeth* symbolism,
a cleansing of the hands from guilt. Equally you may feel he
had good cause for a guilt complex. The way he took the
McSwans, son, mother, and father, into that basement, murdered them and drank their blood: I can see that producing
a guilt complex in most people.

The Hendersons. How he dealt with them! And naïve,
unsuspecting, gullible Mrs. Durand-Deacon.

As Dr. Keith Simpson said in his remarkable paper to the
Society: 'The defence which was put forward—in a case
where the facts undeniably proved a calculated murder for
gain, planned with care and effected with a callous disregard
for feelings *but no small regard for secrecy*—was one of insanity at law.

'Psychiatric assistance in this defence was not lacking, un-
tenable as the proposition might appear to be in law, and the
issue once again raised the adequacy of the McNaughten Rules
as a yardstick by which a lay jury may assess insanity as a
defence on a charge of murder.'

I followed this case from beginning to end and see no reason to alter my view that Haigh was completely sane in law. He robbed his victims. He selected them with some care and malice aforethought. When he was caught, and realised he could hang, he thought of Broadmoor as a refuge from which he could emerge after a decent interval of rehabilitation. In other words, a man who fully appreciated the enormity of his crimes. 'Sane', in every sense of the word that bears on responsibility.

I think he was rightly hanged. Of course, I expect to be attacked for these views. In my own defence, I plead a life-time knowledge of murder and murderers!

Incidentally there is one postscript for us all to ponder. Why is it that in this normally sensible, law abiding and pleasant land of ours we make a habit of producing the world's most savage killers?

In the Latin and Latin American countries and those bordering the Equator, murder is most often the result of passion, a sudden outburst of anger, not premeditated.

In the Middle East—I am not talking about Palestinian refugees and guerrillas—the majority of non-political murders stem from scandal and family dishonour.

In Scandinavian countries, it is traced back too often to an excess of alcohol. The Stockholm crime museum is chock-a-block with axes and woodchoppers and other such weapons any man in that setting—temporarily bereft of his senses—might seize: not premeditated.

In latter years, the U.S.A. has had more than its share of 'weirdie' murders following the huge rise in drug addiction, but even now the gun reigns supreme as murder weapon.

It is left to us in Britain to produce the worst in murder, and murderers: from Jack the Ripper on to child-killers, poisoners, ritual murderers, necrophiliac lovers of long-strangled victims, trunk murderers—and acid bath killers.

# 11  The Lucky Break

It goes without saying that not all murder cases are solved. You can have the best Murder Squad team in the Yard, the most co-operative of local police forces, the public queueing up to make statements—and still draw a blank.

For my money, the loneliest man in the world is a Murder Squad investigator at the start of the trail. He has immense resources at his disposal; he will have a certain number of clues, thin though they may be; and he always has a huge publicity machine, the Fleet Street newspapers, ready and willing to co-operate.

When all that is said, the outcome of every investigation rests very largely on the shoulders of one man, the detective in charge. And there is nothing he needs more than the 'lucky break' to swing the pendulum his way. All his skills, all the patient devotion to duty of his staff, all the brilliant background work of the pathologists—all this can come to naught if his luck is out.

The police investigating the Charing Cross Trunk Murder had this lucky break right at the outset of the case. The speed with which they exploited it and brought the killer to justice makes it rank still as one of the outstanding examples of crime detection on record.

On 6 May, 1927, a cab driver was hailed by a fare in the West End. He wanted to be taken, with his trunk, to Charing Cross station. You don't see many trunks like it today. Then it was fairly commonplace. It was big and made of wicker;

Norman Thorne and Elsie Cameron

Donald Hume (*left*) brings his murder confession to the author

Sidney Fox and his mother

'Mrs Ransom, I believe?' Det. Chief Supt. Peter Beveridge makes his arrest in High Holborn watched by the author

Harry Dobkin and his wife, Rachel

Deputy Commander William Rawlings examines photographs of Mrs Dobkin's skull

Ronald Harries

Det. Chief Supt. John
Capstick (*centre*) at
Harries' Farm

Leslie Green

Det. Chief Supt. (later Commander)
Reginald Spooner on the Green case

John George Haigh

Neville Heath

Chief Constable John E.
Horwell

The author at the graveside of
Mrs Rosse

Kenneth Barlow

Elizabeth Barlow

Arthur Boyce with
Det. Supt. John Ball
who arrested him

Det. Chief Supt. John Du Rose at 'nude murders' H.Q., Shepherds Bush

The author (*right*) with James Callaghan, M.P. then Home Secretary, and Sir Ronald Howe, former head of the C.I.D.

it had a round top, and the whole was covered with black oilcloth; it had two leather 'shoulder pieces' and the middle was secured by a leather strap.

The cabbie helped to load it. The trunk was very heavy. 'Blimey,' said the driver, 'what have you got in 'ere mate? Money?'

'No,' said the fare. 'Books.'

The cab driver forgot it as soon as he pulled away. No-one in the left luggage office paid much attention when it was left or by whom. Five days later they were wishing they had. The stench from the wickerwork trunk was foul and they called in the police.

Detective Inspector Steele, from Bow Street, forced the lid. Inside, covered only by sheets of brown paper, was the dismembered body of a woman. It had been cut into five sections, by amputation at the shoulders and hips.

A call went out for Sir Bernard Spilsbury. He found a large number of bruises, all recently made, and all caused before death. He examined lungs and air passages and gave as cause of death: 'Asphyxia from pressure over mouth and nostrils whilst unconscious from head injury and other injuries.' In other words, she had been knocked out and then suffocated.

There was no clear evidence to her identity. However there were some clues that might help. There was some clothing, including one article which carried a tab bearing the name 'P. Holt'. There were two laundry marks, numbers 581 and 447. Inside the trunk were also a pair of woman's shoes, a duster and an empty handbag. The letters 'I.F.A.' were painted on the trunk. There was also a tie-on label with the words 'F. Austin to St. Lenards' written on it.

They all looked promising. In fact 'F. Austin' had nothing to do with the murder. The mis-spelling of 'St. Leonards' as 'St. Lenards' and the two laundry marks were, however, to play a significant part in its solution.

Murder investigations rarely begin in real life as they once

G

did in movies, with the police arriving in a fleet of cars and the public shooed out of the way so that the ace detective can at once follow up such vital clues.

The Charing Cross Trunk Murder was no exception. I was only a cub crime reporter still (it was just over two years since I had been taken off my showbiz column and sent on my first murder story) but learning fast. One of the first things your newspaper wants to know is how the victim died. Sir Bernard conducted his examination at the mortuary of the Westminster coroner's court, in Horseferry Road, Westminster.

The police questioning began at once at Charing Cross station, one of the busiest in London, with passengers pouring in and out, pushing and shoving—they are always in such a tearing hurry—to the barriers.

At such a time the Fleet Street crime reporter, like Caesar's Gaul, has to be divided into three parts. One part haunting the mortuary, to pick up the vital information about the age of the victim, the method of death—as precisely as the authorities want to be known at the time—and so on. Another part of him has to live on Charing Cross station, questioning the staff, harrying his contacts, gathering a detailed pen picture of the station scene, working closely with his photographer colleagues. The third part must for ever be on the telephone, relaying facts and developments to his news editor. This is no time for journalistic weaklings.

No-one in the left luggage office could remember who booked the trunk in. If that surprises you, bear in mind that they handle something like *two thousand* separate pieces of luggage a day. And right now no-one could tell them when it was handed in.

Then came the million-to-one chance: the lucky break. A shoeblack working on a stand at Charing Cross had come across a screwed-up ball of yellow paper on the ground five days earlier, unravelled it and found it to be a receipt for a piece of luggage. Without thinking, he had slipped it into his pocket.

When the news of the trunk murder broke, he remembered his find, and handed it to the police. Detective Chief Inspector Cornish of the Yard (the same Cornish as in the Furnace case years later) now had a definite time the trunk was deposited.

On this scrap of paper the case was built. From the time factor, the police traced the taxi driver who had brought the trunk to Charing Cross. And *he* remembered the address at which he had picked up the trunk and his fare. Talk about a lucky break!

The tell-tale laundry marks also brought swift results. The clothing came from a house in Chelsea, where some time before a woman known as 'Mrs. Rolls' had worked as cook. Her real name was Minnie Bonati. She was the thirty-six-year-old wife of an Italian waiter. She had been living as 'wife' to a Mr. Rolls. Both men were quickly traced. Neither was responsible for the murder. But the dismembered woman in the trunk was now positively identified.

She was living a fairly promiscuous life. The killer could have been any man she met. But from the taxi driver Cornish now had an address to start from. He got the shock of his life when he went to it. It was right opposite Rochester Row police station.

The man who had hailed the taxi had stood in the doorway of an office block, across the road from the station. Cornish ordered a room by room check. The Murder Squad team found a small estate agency run by a Mr. John Robinson, under the name of Edwards & Co. and operating from a single room, which had just closed down.

On 9 May, three days after the trunk had been deposited at Charing Cross, he had written to the landlords saying:

'Dear Sir, I am sorry to inform you that I have gone broke, so cannot use your office further. Let the people who supplied the typewriter take it away.'

Nothing incriminating was found. But it was vital to trace Mr. Robinson.

Through a bank, Inspector Cornish traced a Camberwell address where Robinson had stayed. It too was searched. Robinson had left, but the police found a letter addressed to him. It was an official Post Office letter saying they had been unable to deliver a telegram he had sent to someone of the same name at the Greyhound Hotel in Hammersmith. A new maid in the hotel, who did not know Mrs. Robinson worked there, had saved the police a lot of footwork and plodding inquiry, by returning the telegram 'Not known here'.

Cornish went to the Greyhound. Mrs. Robinson, who clearly did not know all her husband's movements, was in fact due to meet him that evening, 19 May, at the Elephant and Castle. Cornish kept the rendezvous, and Robinson was taken to the Yard. He talked freely: no, he knew nothing about the Trunk Murder other than facts printed in the newspapers. No, he had no objection whatever to attending an identification parade. His bluff worked.

Neither the taxi driver, the man who sold him the trunk, nor the station porter who had wheeled it into Charing Cross, recognised Robinson.

Cornish felt in his bones he had the right man, but he had no choice: Robinson walked out, a free man. The Murder Squad kept plugging away patiently, checking and re-checking. They went over everything they had found and had heard, time and again.

The effects that had been dropped in the trunk with the remains of Minnie Bonati were examined again. The duster that had been found was deeply bloodstained. Cornish had it washed, in warm soapy water, just on a hunch. When it was dry he could see, sewn on a tab in one corner, the faded word 'Greyhound'.

The Greyhound Hotel!

He wanted more proof, after the failure of that identity parade, and he took his Murder Squad back to the one-room office opposite Rochester Row police station. 'Go over it again,' he said. 'And again. See what you can turn up.'

They spent a day and literally covered the room and its few contents inch by inch. Late in the afternoon Detective Inspector Clarke picked a matchstick out of the wastepaper basket. He turned it over in his fingers and saw that it was slightly discoloured. Tests showed it had a bloodstain, less than an eighth of an inch in size. It was enough (together with the duster) to pin the murder on John Robinson.

Cornish sent two sergeants to pull him in. They woke him at 8 a.m., told him to get dressed and go with them to Scotland Yard. When Cornish arrived to interview him, Robinson talked as freely as before—but more honestly, this time. He had never meant to kill her, he said. He had been accosted by Mrs. Bonati at Victoria Station. They had gone back to his one-roomed office where she had asked for too much money. There was a struggle. She had fallen back and struck her head on the fireplace.

'I left her lying there,' he said. 'I thought she was only stunned.'

Next day he found her—dead—and panicked. He bought a chef's knife at a shop in Victoria, cut her up, buried the knife under a May tree on Clapham Common, and bought a trunk to take the remains to Charing Cross station.

The jury listened to Spilsbury say that the blueness of Mrs. Bonati's finger-nails, and the protruding tongue, were clear indications of suffocation. They rejected Robinson's story and found him guilty as charged. He was later hanged.

Like so many murder stories that have come my way, it was straightforward enough—once all the clues were followed up by quick police action. But the fact that one Charing Cross shoeblack should pick up the one piece of litter at the vital moment in that busy, crowded station to fit them all into place —that was a lucky break to remember.

# 12  The Sadist

The Heath case presented the authorities with a terrible dilemma. Sadist and pervert Neville George Clevely Heath had already committed one murder in London, during which he flogged, bit, suffocated, beat and savagely mutilated a young woman.

He was a monster, wild with desire after gorging on one murder and clearly capable of, and likely to commit, murder again soon. It was absolutely vital to warn the public to be on their guard. The best way of doing that, in 1946, was to issue his picture to the newspapers.

The police were able to do it: Heath had a record and they had a photograph of him in the files. *But* the only positive evidence they had that Heath had accompanied the woman to the hotel where she was murdered came from a cab driver who took them as fare. And here was the dilemma: if Heath's picture appeared in the newspapers before the trial, the defence would almost certainly maintain the taxi driver had been unduly influenced by its publication. In plain English, defence counsel would infer he was claiming to recognise a face he had only seen in the newspapers. On that, a case could founder.

So a calculated gamble was taken that Heath's photograph would be circulated to the police only, in the hope and belief that someone, somewhere in uniform would pick him up before he murdered again.

The gamble failed. That decision cost another life, for Heath did murder a second time. No-one knows if that life would have been spared had the alternative course been taken—of saying, publish and be damned!—but it is possible, even likely. That was a hideous dilemma for all those CID chiefs saddled with the responsibility of decision. Their feelings when the news of the second murder broke can be imagined.

A curious sideline to the Heath case is that Fleet Street's reporters knew Heath well, under one name or another, long before the murders. We didn't like him whatever the label he wore. Incidentally, one world famous figure who thoroughly distrusted him is Denis Compton the former international cricketer and footballer, born—like me—at Bridport. Denis, who of course is now a colleague of mine on the *Sunday Express,* rated Heath a dangerous phoney.

World War 2 had just ended. Millions were still in uniform, and it was fashionable in many quarters for temporary officers and gentlemen to cling to their wartime rank even when demobbed. The pubs were packed with returning warriors, and the hangar doors were open in every saloon bar every day. In Fleet Street we suffered 'Group Captain Armstrong' almost daily. The dashing Groupie, alias Heath, was such an obvious exhibitionist, such a patent fraud to us old cynics. It has always been a source of amazement to me that women should fall so easily—and fatally—for his brittle, surface charm.

Our instinct was right, our suspicious noses had caught the right scent. Ladies' man Heath was in fact a brute, a sadist, and quite horrific killer. Now his blood was roused, and he was prowling through the hotels and pubs of London like any animal in the jungle looking for prey.

On the night of 20 June, 1946, Neville Heath was drinking and dancing with thirty-two-year-old Mrs. Margery Gardner at the Panama Club in South Kensington, in London. Mrs. Gardner was an experienced young woman who liked men. Heath fascinated her, with his crinkly blond hair, pale blue

eyes and baby-smooth skin. Around midnight they left the
Panama, with many a drink on board, and took a cab to the
Pembridge Court Hotel in the Notting Hill district. Heath had
booked in there some days before with another girl friend,
whom he allowed to leave quite unharmed, and had signed
the register 'Lt. Colonel & Mrs. N. G. C. Heath'.

He still had a front door key to the hotel from that booking,
so on the night he arrived late with Mrs. Gardner no-one
in the hotel ever heard them or saw them together. *The only
witness to their arrival together was the taxi driver who brought
them from the Panama Club.*

At two o'clock the next afternoon the chambermaid used
her master key and went into the bedroom they had used after
knocking two or three times without answer. One twin bed
was soaked in blood. In the other lay the body of Mrs. Gardner, with sheets drawn up to her neck. The 'colonel' was
missing.

Detective Inspector Shelley Symes and pathologist Dr.
Keith Simpson were called to the hotel. It was clearly a sex
murder and the work of a maniac. Her ankles were still tied
together, and her face and body, front and back, were covered
in bloody weals. They appeared to have been made with a
metal-tipped cane or riding crop. Her face was severely bruised
consistent with blows from a clenched fist, and there were
more bruises on her throat, as though strangulation had been
attempted. (It was later proved that suffocation with a pillow
was the actual cause of death.) Her face had been washed
before the killer left—why was never clear.

A hunt was started for 'Colonel Heath'. His background
was interesting. His schooldays were shared between a Roman
Catholic school and grammar school, which he left at the age
of seventeen. Date of birth: 1917. Place: Ilford, Essex.

In February 1936 he obtained a short-service commission in
the Royal Air Force. He won his wings as pilot, but the next
year he was dismissed the Service for a number of civil
offences. He stole an NCO's car, went absent without leave and

'bounced' a few cheques. After he was dismissed from the Air Force, he went around posing as 'Lord Dudley'—rank and title always seemed to fascinate Heath—and bounced more cheques, whereupon he was placed on probation for two years. In the summer of 1938 he was sent to Borstal for housebreaking.

He was sentenced to three years there, but was released on the outbreak of war so that he could volunteer for the Armed Forces. He did so at once. He joined the Army this time, and by March 1940 he was once more an officer and a gentleman (so much for Selection Boards!) and was posted to Cairo. But Heath just could not keep out of trouble. There followed one escapade after another. Then, in July 1941, after swindling the Paymaster into paying him two salaries as Captain and disappearing without leave into the fleshpots of Egypt, Heath was courtmartialled and dismissed the Service *a second time*!

Most Armies would have flung a man in jail for this, but not ours: not an officer. On 27 October, 1941, *Mister* Heath, civilian, sailed from Egypt (second class, naturally, following his disgrace and dismissal) on the s.s. *Mooltan,* bound for Old Blighty's shores via Durban. Life on board ship clearly agreed with Heath. I have a sharply descriptive eyewitness report from Wing Commander Johnny Johnston, who sailed with Heath on the *Mooltan.* Wing Commander Johnston wrote to me about Heath in April, 1970:

'Heath was a handsome young man at that time, and it was obvious that some women on board were attracted to him. It may have been his good looks and aloof manner which attracted *them,* but he struck me at the time as being a very suave and plausible rogue.

'He left the ship at Durban, driven off in a large car by a well-dressed and attractive lady. The ship stayed there for three weeks, *and during that time we had inquiries from the South African police about Heath.*

'As far as I can recall now, their inquiries concerned a

road accident where the body of a woman had been found
in a burned-out car.

'Heath never joined the ship for the rest of the voyage.'

Incredibly, Heath enlisted again. This time he volunteered
for the South African Air Force, where he served for a trouble-
free rest-of-the-war record. He collected a wife on the way.
Neville Heath married in South Africa in 1942. Very little is
known about the marriage. But Mrs. Heath divorced him in
October 1945, while he was away serving with S.A.A.F.

Heath was by all accounts a good pilot and aircrew officer:
but he could not stay out of mischief on the ground. On 4
December, 1945, the South Africans made it number three—
and cashiered him for a number of offences. I don't know
if Heath's is a unique military record, to be thrown out of
the service of the Crown three times in eight years, but it
certainly is unique in the criminal world.

He came back to England in February 1946. Two months
later he was in court. He was fined £10 by the Wimbledon
magistrates for wearing uniform and ribbons he had no right
to wear. Now he was officially a phoney, and it was at this
time that 'Group Captain Armstrong, D.S.O.' was trying to
strike up friendships in Fleet Street.

Now there was a naked, mutilated body lying in a bed in the
Pembridge Court Hotel, and Heath had committed murder.

And now it was that the authorities had to make that fateful
decision: to issue his picture to the newspapers or not. They
did not. Instead they put out a statement and his description,
saying the police were anxious to contact him 'in case he
could help their inquiries'.

Heath was moving quietly around the southern seaside
resorts, Brighton, Angmering, Worthing. He booked into the
Ocean Hotel in Worthing. Then, cool as you like, he rang the
same young woman who had spent the night with him at the
Pembridge Court Hotel four days before the murder.

Naturally, she raised the subject of murder—in their hotel,

*in their room.* The story was in every newspaper. She could talk of little else. 'Colonel Heath' said yes, indeed, it was awful, but you see he had simply lent his door-key to a couple who wanted privacy and had slept elsewhere on the night himself.

Colonel Heath called on the girl at home. The visit was not an unqualified success. Her parents did not care much for him. And when they too read in the newspapers that Heath was wanted—merely for questioning in case he could help inquiries—they made their daughter *insist* he contacted the authorities. Perhaps by so doing they saved her life. Perhaps the Fiend of Notting Hill intended her no harm: who knows? But either way there walks a lucky, lucky woman today.

Heath said goodbye to her. He never went to London. Instead he went to the Tollard Royal Hotel in Bournemouth and registered as 'Group Captain Rupert Brooke'. However, before he left Worthing, he sat down and wrote a long letter to the CID chief in London who was directing the manhunt for him. It was a curious thing to do. It was a curious letter, too, tantamount to an invitation to the police to pull him in for questioning. He even told them how to get in touch with him: via the personal column of the *Daily Telegraph.*

He may have written because the young lady had urged him so strongly to get in touch with the police. It may have been intended as another lie, another red herring. There may have been, though personally I doubt it, a noble motive behind the letter. Eminent counsel certainly thought so. After his trial Joshua Casswell, K.C., for the defence, said he believed Heath wished to be prevented from killing again.

Heath wrote to Det. Superintendent Tom Barratt:

'Sir,
'I feel it to be my duty to inform you of certain facts in connection with the death of Mrs. Gardner at Notting Hill Gate.
'I booked in at the hotel last Sunday, but not with Mrs.

Gardner, whom I met for the first time during the week. I had drinks with her on Friday evening, and whilst I was with her she met an acquaintance with whom she was obliged to sleep.

'The reasons, as I understand them, were mainly financial. It was then that Mrs. Gardner asked if she could use my hotel room until two o'clock, and intimated that if I returned after that, I might spend the remainder of the night with her.

'I gave her my keys and told her to leave the hotel door open. It must have been almost 3 a.m. when I returned to the hotel, and found her in the condition of which you are aware.

'I realised that I was in an invidious position, and rather than notify the police, I packed my belongings and left. Since then I have been in several minds whether to come forward or not, but in view of the circumstances I have been afraid to.

'I can give you a description of the man. He was aged approx. 30, dark hair, black, with small moustache. Height about 5ft. 9in. slim build. His name was Jack, and I gathered he was a friend of Mrs. Gardner of some long standing.

'The personal column of the *Daily Telegraph* will find me but at the moment I have assumed another name. I should like to come forward and help, but I cannot face the music of a fraud charge which will obviously be preferred against me if I should do so.

'I have the instrument with which Mrs. Gardner was beaten and am forwarding this to you today.

'You will find my finger prints on it, but you should also find others as well.

signed,<br>
N. G. C. Heath.'

He never sent the riding crop to Superintendent Barratt or anyone else at the Yard. The letter was interesting: Heath was sounding out the police with an alibi. There is no sign of insanity, read it how you will.

The letter was received in London on 24 June. From then until 3 July, while his picture was circulated to every police station in the country but none shown to the unsuspecting public, Heath lived quite openly as Group Captain Rupert Brooke at the Tollard Royal. Down on the front he found his next victim, an ex-Wren called Doreen Marshall.

Doreen was a fine young woman, pretty, well brought up, and on holiday alone because she was recovering from a bad bout of 'flu. There was no mystery about how she met Heath: a smile from the dashing blond young man, a casual word on a sunny morning, a date for dinner that night—and murder.

He entertained her to dinner at his hotel and they had drinks in the lounge afterwards. As on the night he murdered Mrs. Gardner, Heath was drinking hard all night. Miss Marshall tried to get a cab back to her own hotel, Heath insisted they walk—and he would escort her. She agreed. She was never seen alive again.

Before they left, Heath told the night porter he would be back shortly. He did not use the hotel entrance, but climbed a builder's ladder instead and got into his room unseen by the staff.

The night porter, a conscientious man, kept an eye on the clock. At 4.30 a.m. he went into Heath's room—and saw him asleep in bed. He noted that Heath's shoes were in the room, by the bed, and caked with sand, instead of being out in the corridor for cleaning. Heath admitted coming in by ladder, next morning.

Two days went by before Miss Marshall was missed at her hotel. The manager made inquiries. Someone remembered she had a dinner date at the Tollard on 3 July. When *his* hotel manager questioned him, Heath denied his guest had been Doreen Marshall.

Her body was discovered by a woman, out with her dog in the bushes and flowers of Bournemouth's Branksome Chine. She was naked. Her dress and underclothes were placed on top of her body. Her stockings were found yards away. She had been badly beaten, stabbed, and disgustingly mutilated. The worst mutilations were made after death. The police believed Heath stripped naked himself before the attack and that this explains the lack of bloodstains on his clothing. And that he washed himself clean in the sea after the murder, dressed and walked back to his hotel.

Heath had physically to walk right into a police station and confront a man in uniform before he was recognised, but by then it was too late to prevent another murder, too late to help poor Doreen Marshall.

All my life as a crime reporter I have tried to see the police point of view and I do not criticise them now: I merely question, as I have always done, the decision to withhold general publication of his picture.

Apart from the letter to Det. Superintendent Barratt, there was no clue to Heath's whereabouts. Heath put his own head in the noose. When Doreen Marshall was still officially missing he rang the police in Bournemouth (as Group Captain Rupert Brooke) and offered to help them in their inquiries.

They accepted. When the handsome, blue-eyed Group Captain strolled round to the station, a sharp-eyed young detective thought he bore an uncanny resemblance to a wanted man called Heath. He held him pending further inquiries and called the Murder Squad. When they found the body next day, Heath was already in the bag.

Spooner of the Yard (a Detective Inspector in 1946) questioned Heath. On his arrival Spooner had been handed a statement Heath had written and again it was interesting, fascinating even—he was accused of nothing yet here he was offering another alibi.

He wrote that Miss Marshall (*on the dinner night, at the Tollard*),

'told me she was considering cutting short her holiday in Bournemouth and returning home on Friday. She mentioned an American staying in her hotel, and told me he had taken her for car rides. She also mentioned an invitation to go with him to Exeter but I gathered—although she did not actually say so—that she did not intend to go.

'Another American was mentioned, I believe his name was Pat, to whom I believe she was unofficially engaged some while ago.

'At 11 p.m. Miss Marshall suggested going away but I persuaded her to stay a little longer. About 11.30 the weather was clear and we left the hotel and sat on a seat, overlooking the sea.

'From this stage onward my times were vague because I had no wristwatch. We must have talked for at least an hour, probably longer, and then we walked down the slope to the Pavilion. Miss Marshall did not wish me to accompany her but I insisted on doing so at least part of the way.

'I left her at the pier and watched her cross the road and enter the gardens.

'Before leaving I asked her if she would come round the following day, but she said she would be busy for the next few days, but would telephone me on Sunday, if she could manage it.

'I have not seen her to speak to since then, although I thought I saw her entering Bobby's Ltd. on Thursday morning.

'After leaving Miss Marshall, I walked along the seafront in a westerly direction and up the path from Durley Chine, and to the clifftop, and so back to the hotel where I went to bed.

'It rained heavily before I reached the hotel.'

Spooner took Heath back to London. After attending an identity parade he was picked out by the cab driver who had taken him and Mrs. Gardner to their Notting Hill Gate hotel. Heath was then charged with Mrs. Gardner's murder. He made no reply.

He was tried at the Old Bailey in September that year, before Mr. Justice Morris. Heath's counsel pleaded insanity and called Dr. William Hubert, psychiatrist and former psychotherapist at Broadmoor, for the defence.

Heath himself would have none of it. Halfway through the doctor's evidence Heath scribbled this note from the dock to his counsel: 'It may be of interest to know that in my discussions with Hubert I have never suggested that I should be excused or that I told him I felt I should be, because of insanity.'

Very few madmen, of course, believe themselves insane so Heath's protest was not inconsistent with his counsel's plea.

Joshua Casswell pleaded that Heath was 'as mad as a hatter'. And there are those who believed Heath actually murdered Doreen Marshall in a deliberate attempt to escape the hangman (for the Mrs. Gardner murder) by being sent to Broadmoor.

The judge had this to say:

'The tests as to insanity to which I have referred are the tests which have in all criminal cases to be applied in regard to this matter. Whether medical men might wish from a medical point of view to frame other tests is not a question with which I need trouble you.

'We are here to administer the law.

'Equally you will see that insanity is not to be found merely because some conduct might be regarded as so outrageous as to be wholly unexpected from the generality of men.

'Strong sexual instinct is not insanity: a mere love of bloodshed or mere recklessness are not in themselves insanity: an inability to resist temptation, the satisfaction of some perverted impulse, is not, without more, to be excused on the ground of insanity.

'The plea of insanity cannot be permitted to become the easy or vague explanation of some conduct which is shocking merely because it is startling.

'The law of insanity is not to become the refuge of those who cannot challenge a charge which is brought against them.'

I sat in the court and listened to the Judge very carefully. Already we were moving into the fringe battlefield of the capital punishment issue, though none of us realised it so clearly then, and I would have liked his words to be hung on the wall of every defence counsel and psychiatrist in the land.

Heath was sentenced to death. He was hanged at Pentonville, on 16 October, 1946.

Heath died coolly enough. When the prison Governor paid his final call and offered this fresh-faced, scrubbed-looking, so-handsome young man a last drink (of brandy), Heath rustled up a grin from somewhere and jokingly asked for a double. He got it. And went straightway to his death on the scaffold.

I shed no tears for the sadist Heath. But still, today, a quarter of a century later, I could weep at the decision that had to be made within the requirements of the law and led directly to the murder of Doreen Marshall. If the public had been warned, she need not have died: the likelihood is that Heath would have been recognised by some member of the public long before he could have killed a second time.

I had long talks with my friends in the CID over this (Spooner was one of them) and I know how they grieved over the Marshall murder. But is there a dry-as-dust official mind that could not care less as long as the letter of the law is obeyed?

After the case was over, I published the official picture of Heath as it appeared in the *Police Gazette*. I said this was the picture every policeman carried in his uniform pocket—but none of the public were allowed to see.

I was later told that the Director of Public Prosecutions had 'seriously' considered summoning me for 'publishing an official document'. For the sake of the police and the reputation of the Yard, I am glad he did not. That would have made a bad decision contemptuous.

H

# 13  The Derby Winner

I doubt if the prestige of the Yard was ever higher than in the Roaring Twenties. Elsewhere in the world, the police image was poor, even downright bad: in America for instance. Police efficiency, which we took for granted here in Britain, was a joke in some of the poorer countries of the world.

The Yard's high reputation was based squarely on crime-breaking and incorruptibility. It was richly deserved. In those early days as a crime reporter, I was privileged to know and work with the best that the Yard could produce, and among those, the élite were to be found in the Murder Squad.

One man who walked tall throughout his career was John Horwell, who made his way up from the beat to become head of the CID and finally Chief Constable of the Yard. I first met him in 1928, when I was already gaining some reputation as a crime reporter (my first years had proved very lucky), and we became good friends.

He was a Chief Inspector at the time. He was everything you looked for in the police image: wholly incorruptible, shrewd, blessed with a filing-cabinet of a mind, enormous patience, an ability to co-ordinate the efforts of a Murder Squad so that not a moment was wasted in the whole range of inquiry. He came from an old school but he was always alert to the advances of forensic science: Johnny Horwell used everything and everyone about him in the prosecution of a case.

But, being old school, he never forgot his 'homework'. He

knew the value of the old hands who represented a living storehouse of information on the small-time crooks and petty thieves of London. He was a stickler for routine, the patient house-to-house check, the sifting of reports from every divisional station.

All these qualities paid dividends in quick time after the Bayswater shooting of hotel owner Bertram Webb.

Mr. Webb drove home to his flat in Pembridge Square on a raw winter's evening in February 1928 with his eighteen-year-old son Clifford and a friend named Frank Sweeney.

The gas lamps were alight when he parked outside the house. Upstairs on the landing outside Webb's flat they saw glass fragments scattered on the carpet. A glass panel was smashed over the lock. They looked through, into the flat and saw the outline of a man wearing a bowler hat silhouetted against the window. They thought they had the burglar trapped.

'Run for the police, Cliff!' shouted Bertram Webb and went in to tackle him. The other two ran down the stairs to get help. They heard a man shout 'Put 'em up!' in the time-honoured gunman's phrase, and they ran with wings on their feet for they thought he was aiming at them.

As they turned into the street they heard the muffled *crack* of a pistol shot. Clifford Webb turned back to help his father. He caught a fleeting glimpse of a man running out of the doorway. He found his father lying on the stairs, blood pouring from a close-range wound in the head.

Mr. Webb, who was unconscious, died the next morning in St. Mary's hospital. He did not regain consciousness. There was no description of the killer.

Chief Inspector Horwell was sent down to investigate the murder. He found all the hallmarks of a professional housebreaker caught redhanded on the job: attaché case half-filled with silver and valuables, signs of a panicky getaway. While his finger-print men and photographers went through the flat, Horwell sent his team of investigators to knock on every door in Pembridge Square. They had orders to find every person who had been in the square around five-thirty the previous evening.

Within a very short time they recovered the murder weapon. One man had nearly been knocked over by the intruder as he ran down the street. 'I saw him throw something into one of the gardens,' he told the police. A search produced a .32 automatic pistol. Laboratory tests showed the man who fired it had worn gloves and there were no fingerprints.

Horwell went back to the beginning and started again. Use of firearms, always a rarity in Britain in the 'twenties, was quite exceptional in the context of housebreaking. So Horwell left that aside for the moment and concentrated all his inquiries on the commonplace—known housebreakers and a study of their methods.

'Find out,' he told his men, 'if anyone was sounding the drum on the day of the shooting.'

*Sounding the drum* is a lazy and haphazard run-up to breaking and entering. You don't 'case' a selected property, carefully noting the movements of the people inside, and choose a time to break in when you are reasonably sure the coast is clear. You just choose any likely-looking district, walk up to a house and ring the bell. If no-one comes to the door, your luck is in—the place is empty, you smash a window and take a chance. *If* someone answers your ring, you use your wits: think up a quick excuse and move on to another house to try again.

Someone *had* been sounding the drum in Pembridge Square that day: a man in a bowler hat. About 5 p.m. he called at one house where no lights were showing and rang the bell. He was unlucky: someone was in, an old lady sitting by the fire, curtains drawn and no chink of light visible in the street.

She came to the door and asked what the man in the bowler hat wanted. 'The chauffeur,' he said quickly. 'Is he in, madam?'

There was no chauffeur. She said as much.

'I'm sorry,' said the caller. 'I must have come to the wrong address.'

If he had turned on his heel and walked away there and then, the man in the bowler might never have been caught and hanged. But he lingered. The old lady spoke to him again.

'Where have you come from?' she asked.

'The Warwick garage,' he answered. Then he left.

The old lady repeated his words to the detectives who called later. She was able to describe him. A little man, she said, of her own height even with the bowler on: that made him about five feet tall.

Horwell called all the 'old hands' from the Divisions in London into conference with his Murder Squad. He put the few known facts before them. Then he told them how they could help.

'The *Warwick* garage,' he said. 'Does it mean anything? Why would someone sounding the drum think of that name? Any ideas? Do you know anyone in your manor with any form who is called Warwick? Lives in Warwick Road or Warwick Street? Married to a girl of that name? Come on, *think.*'

One detective sergeant from Notting Hill knew a pint-sized housebreaker who could fit the bill. Name, Frederick Stewart; occupation, bookie's clerk; and with relatives living in Warwick Road.

Horwell checked with Records. There was no previous record of violence. He ordered Stewart to be brought in for questioning, none the less. Stewart was nowhere to be found in London. Horwell learned he was an inveterate gambler, favoured the dogs, and had a distinct preference for the track at Southend-on-Sea.

I moved with the Murder Squad down to Southend—it was cold and bleak at the time. They checked the greyhound track, the bookies, the pubs, the boarding houses, without success.

On what was to be their last night in Southend, a detective sergeant called Welsby and two colleagues paid a last call at a pub near the pier. Sergeant Welsby pushed open the door of the saloon bar, quickly, to get out of the biting wind; it bumped against a customer inside and spilled his beer. The customer was five feet tall and his name was Frederick Stewart.

John Horwell would never admit that as lucky: he felt it was routine investigation paying off. 'Maybe a little of both,' I told him when we met over a glass of whisky later.

Stewart was taken back to London and charged. He never denied being in the Webbs' flat, but he refused to admit to murder. It was an accident, he said. The gun went off in the struggle when they found him.

It was left to a jury to decide. They refused to believe Stewart and found him guilty. He was sentenced to death and later hanged.

He showed a remarkable aplomb while he waited in the death cell for the hangman to call. Instead of playing cards or dominoes with his warders, as so many condemned men did to while away the weeks of waiting for possible reprieve, he spent his time poring over the racing form book.

His execution was set for 6 June: Derby Day.

I still can't make up my mind if little Frederick Stewart had nerves of steel or was simply devoid of normal imagination: but he actually asked the prison governor if his hanging could be postponed for a day so that he could be told the result of the big race!

Request refused. He was hanged at 8 a.m., seven hours before the 'Off'. As he was led to the scaffold, he gave a last tip.

'Have a few bob on Felstead today,' he said.

It won, at 33 to 1.

# 14  Clues to a Killer

In all my time as attendant to the crime of murder, I have never known a killer leave more clues to his identity and whereabouts than Henry Daniel Seymour.

He:  left his card at the scene of the crime;
     called at a pub immediately after the murder and told everyone where he would spend the night;
     dumped the murder weapon (a hammer), left means of identifying the shopkeeper who sold it to him; and threw in as a bonus—
     his hideout address and alias he had adopted.

I hardly need to add that Henry Seymour was quickly caught and hanged. But the clues unfolded in the manner of a crossword puzzle, each dependent on the one before: with the first so hard to find it was nearly overlooked.

On a clammy August Bank holiday night in 1931, my old friend Chief Inspector John Horwell was once more called out on the murder trail. This time to Oxford, to investigate the slaying of Mrs. Annie Louisa Kempson, a widow of fifty-eight.

She lived in The Boundary, in St. Clement's Street. Her late husband was a tradesman in the university town and had left her comfortably off, owner of the house she lived in. Mrs. Kempson also had a woman lodger, and she was in the foolish habit of keeping sums of money about the house.

She should have arrived at her brother's house in London on the Saturday starting the holiday weekend. Now it was Monday, there was no sign of her, and her brother was hammering on the door of her house in Oxford to find out what was wrong.

Miss Williams, the lodger, was away for the weekend. Her brother went round the house, saw that the rooms had been ransacked and picked up a stone to break a window and force his way in. He found his sister, covered with a rug and several cushions, dead on the floor of the dining room. He called the Oxford police. Soon afterwards John Horwell was on his way from the Yard, complete with murder bag.

It was clearly murder in the course of robbery. Fingerprint and photographic experts went to work inside The Boundary and teams of sweating policemen began searching the garden. Methodical as ever, Horwell put in an immediate call to Sir Bernard Spilsbury to come down and say what he found. There was a lost weekend to account for. Horwell wanted to know above all *when* she died.

Spilsbury set to work at once. Head wounds—the first coming from behind, giving the widow no chance to defend herself. The attack seemed to have started inside the front hall. As the blows followed, Mrs. Kempson either stumbled or was carried into the dining room where her assailant finished his grisly task by driving a sharp-edged weapon into her neck.

Vicious, premeditated murder. When had it been committed?

The stomach contents pinpointed Mrs. Kempson's last meal, and that put the murder on Saturday morning. Horwell knew something else about the person who came to kill that Saturday: he had not broken into the house. There was no sign of forced entry, apart from the window pane Mrs. Kempson's brother had broken. Whoever had killed her had been invited into The Boundary.

There was no trace of the murder weapon. Horwell's men worked right through the night and next day, searching the house, and still found no lead.

Horwell was a hard driver. In his own words: 'We all worked day and night throughout that period, seldom getting more than an hour or two for sleep, and missing our meals, which we snatched at odd times. As far as my own staff was concerned, one of them . . . nearly died'.

Then came the break. One of the Oxford detectives seconded to the Murder Squad searched the dining room again, inch by inch. He managed to move a mantel over the fireplace: and a visiting card fluttered down to the floor.

It read: 'Mr. Henry Seymour, area manager, St. Margaret's Road, Oxford.' The address had been pencilled out. 'Thorncliffe Road' was substituted.

Horwell was a walking encyclopedia on names and records of smalltime crooks, housebreakers in particular, and the name *Seymour* clicked into place at once. He had a record of violence: two years earlier he had been charged with maliciously wounding an old woman in Paignton, Devon. In those days, he had been working as a door-to-door vacuum cleaner salesman.

Inquiries at the two Oxford addresses revealed that Seymour had left the area two months before the murder. No-one knew where he had moved from there. So Horwell redoubled his questioning in and around St. Clement's Street to find out if anyone had seen Seymour in the area that Saturday.

Neighbour Tom Hall recalled that a man answering to Seymour's description had knocked on the front door of The Boundary at 10 a.m. on Saturday. He was seen following Mrs. Kempson into the house after a brief conversation.

Another woman remembered the man—or someone very much like him—walking near the house at eleven o'clock and looking 'very agitated'.

Down at the local pub they remembered a stranger coming in that morning looking dazed—'as if he'd been in a car accident,' said one—and buying a drink. Before he left he told the barman he was going to catch the bus to Aylesbury, and so he did.

Horwell's men swarmed into Aylesbury, with orders to check every hotel and boarding house. They found the hotel where he had stayed and left without paying the bill—so he was well remembered. His luggage had been impounded.

In it the Murder Squad found a complete set of burglar's tools, plus a hammer and a sharp-edged chisel. Fragments of a paper label from the hammer were found in Seymour's bag. They were traced to an ironmonger's shop near The Boundary and there the shopkeeper remembered selling both hammer and chisel to a man resembling Seymour on Friday—the night before the murder.

The crime reporters from Fleet Street were camped in force at Aylesbury. The hunt for Seymour was making headlines with each new clue that came to light. But none of us imagined he would leave his forwarding address. In the luggage, Horwell's men came across a half-filled crossword puzzle. Below the puzzle was an address in Brighton and the name 'Harvey'. Horwell telephoned the Brighton CID. A watch was set on the address and, sure enough, Harvey turned out to be Seymour.

Henry Daniel Seymour protested his innocence, but the subsequent trial went steadily against him. The defence called a number of witnesses who swore they had seen Mrs. Kempson out alive and shopping on Saturday afternoon (the day of the murder). One thought she had seen the elderly widow posting a letter, but no-one was ever found who had received such a letter.

Spilsbury's evidence was damning as ever.

A piece of cloth wrapped round the hammer and struck into a board produced marks of exactly the same size as Annie Kempson's headwounds.

The sharp-edged chisel, bought—like the hammer—from the Oxford ironmonger's shop on the night before the murder exactly matched the type of weapon used to stab her in the neck.

And, to be sure, there was even the visiting card. Seymour, who was married and had a wife living in Oxford, had sold a vacuum cleaner to Mrs. Kempson several months before the murder. She had kept his card in case the machine ever needed repairs.

Seymour made very little out of the murder. He stole a few pounds from the widow's handbag but overlooked a cardboard box filled with notes and jewellery.

Incidentally, with the help of those clues, it took John Horwell just two weeks to trace and arrest Seymour for the murder of Mrs. Kempson. I have always believed that by his speed he prevented another Seymour murder. For when the police searched his Brighton rooms, they discovered he had bored two holes through the floor (with a chisel!) to keep watch on his landlady below.

Now, he wasn't a Peeping Tom. Seymour wasn't that sort of man.

He was lying down on that floor, squinting and straining into the room below, every time his landlady moved—to see where she kept her money. And I have not the slightest doubt he would have murdered her, just as he had killed widow Kempson, but for a visiting card tucked under a mantel in Oxford, and the tenacity of a detective called Horwell.

# 15  Getting Away with Murder

I can smell a con-man a mile off. Maundy Gregory was the biggest, the smoothest, the most impressive, the *grandest* I ever met. He could fix you up with a title—for the right amount—and managed it for a number of people.

He could introduce you to an Archbishop or a Cabinet minister. He knew the generals and the admirals, and he knew how to play on their vanity. He hoodwinked kings and queens, and persuaded the exiled Montenegrin royal family to grant him power of attorney.

Maundy Gregory always used black blotting paper. Straight-faced, he told his clients this was so that no-one could read what he had written by holding *his* blotter to the mirror!

He toted around a pedigree, a family tree which traced his line of descent direct to Edward III. In circles that were greedy for honours, and willing to pay cash for titles, such things were very impressive. Mr. Gregory forgot to mention his eighty-year-old mother, who sat counting her pennies in a Winchester almshouse.

He worked from posh offices slap in Whitehall and kidded many into believing he was head of our Secret Service. There wasn't a diplomat at the Court of St. James who did not know Maundy Gregory, in those golden, crazy, anything-goes days of the middle 'thirties.

Maundy Gregory was a magnificent con man. There is also a distinct possibility that he was a poisoner who got away with murder.

There is no doubt whatever that the certificate recording the death in Maundy Gregory's house of the actress Mrs. Edith Marion Rosse, on 11 September, 1932, was false in every detail. It stated she died of a stroke, caused by cerebral haemorrhage and Bright's Disease. During the final stages of her illness, whatever it was, Edith Rosse had a new will made out—in Gregory's handwriting—leaving all her money, more than £18,000—a very considerable sum in those days—to Gregory!

Her body was later exhumed. Sir Bernard Spilsbury made the examination. He found no sign of brain haemorrhage, no trace of Bright's Disease. Which, of course, automatically posed a further question: just how did Mrs. Rosse die after conveniently leaving Mr. Gregory all that money?

The police looked, and looked expectantly, for traces of poison. They found none, and thereby hangs a curious and you may think significant tale. But let us start with a look at this astonishing character John Maundy Gregory.

He was the sort of man, I think, who could have flourished only in the P. G. Wodehouse Britain of the 'thirties: pompous, snobridden, class-conscious. In those days men thought they could buy respectability with a title. Maundy Gregory found a way of supplying them—and in no time at all he had a long queue of clients, each with a fortune in his hand, waiting outside his office door.

The going prices were £10,000 for a knighthood, £20,000 for a baronetcy, £50,000 for a peerage. You think I exaggerate? Well, I know of one very rich chain store proprietor who wrote out a cheque for £50,000 made out to Maundy Gregory and signed 'X'. He told Gregory: 'I will accept your proposition. Here is my cheque made out for £50,000 in the name of "X"—*the title I have decided to adopt.* You can cash the cheque the day I receive the peerage.'

I called on Gregory in his palatial Whitehall offices about this time and interviewed him. It was all very impressive. He had an almost unbearable air of conceit about him: he sniffed his disdain at meeting a humble *reporter* and continually dropped hints about having to 'pop over to Number 10' and to 'the Palace' to impress me. He took good care I should notice the twinkling diamond chain that lay across his ample waist-coat. His messengers all wore uniform so akin to Government office uniform it was almost a forgery. Many were ex-Service-men, laden with ribbons, and by their presence lent an air of decency and authority to the Gregory rooms that was doubly impressive.

Gregory was always too busy to see callers on time. I waited nearly an hour before the light flashed on-off-on to let me know he was back from 'Buckingham Palace' and could see me—at last.

The summons issued by the Public Prosecutor charging Gregory with an offence under the Honours (Prevention of Abuses) Act was served in February 1933. It was the begin-ning of the end for this little man who was a staunch friend and confidant of ex-King George of Greece, and who actually wielded power of attorney for Prince Danilo and his wife, the exiled Montenegrin royal pair.

Gregory was found out and the 'Honours Scandal' that threatened to break with his appearance at Bow Street seemed certain to rock the country. Big political names had to be involved with any man who laid claim to 'fixing' titles. It was alleged that Gregory 'unlawfully attempted to obtain the sum of £10,000 from Lt. Cdr. Edward Whaney Leake, DSO, RN retd., of Lowndes Square S.W. as an inducement for endeav-ouring to procure the grant of a dignity or title of honour for Lt. Cdr. Leake . . . contrary to the Honours Act'.

The gallant commander's story was sheer political dynamite. He said he had been introduced to Gregory who explained that certain high authorities wanted Leake to have some kind of honour bestowed but that 'sinews would be necessary to open certain closed doors'. In plain English, a bribe was needed.

Gregory, he said, boasted of arranging many similar transac-tions, and if the Commander liked to give him £10,000 (£12,000 would be better) he could be helped too. Commander

Leake went straight to the police and Gregory was duly charged.

As I said, the implications were pure political dynamite, but the Bow Street hearing turned out to be a most fortunate damp squib for the authorities. Gregory withdrew his early plea of 'not guilty'. The case was all over within a few minutes, without a single political secret being uncovered or an intrigue revealed. Gregory got two months and was ordered to pay a fine of £50 and the costs of the prosecution. Further attempts to raise the Honours Scandal in Parliament remained mysteriously but firmly bogged down.

*Mrs. Rosse's exhumation was ordered while he was serving the two months' jail sentence.*

Gregory always denied that Edith Rosse was his mistress. She was fifty-nine when she died on 11 September, 1932. For ten years or so she had been separated from her husband, Frederick Rosse the conductor and composer, and for all that time she lived in a house in St. John's Wood, in London, where she passed herself off as Gregory's sister.

She told some of her relatives just before she died that Maundy Gregory was hard up and pressing her for money. She mentioned that she had torn up an earlier will at his suggestion. They warned her not to be too trusting. They were distinctly unhappy about her last will and testament, made out on the back of a restaurant menu *in Gregory's handwriting* stating baldly:

'Everything I have to be left to Mr. J. Maundy Gregory to be disposed of as he thinks best, and in accordance of what I should desire.'

And there was the sudden, dramatic death to follow—with all the cash made over so coveniently to the hard-pushed Honours fixer. It was too much. The relatives went to the police and passed on their fears and suspicions.

So the exhumation was ordered. Now here was a most curious thing. Mrs. Rosse had been buried in an unsealed coffin at Bisham, near Maidenhead, a riverbank churchyard continually subject to flooding: thus she lay in a waterlogged grave, *ideally suited to destroy all trace of certain poisons.* And she had been hurriedly put there, on Gregory's personal instructions.

I remember well how the water streamed out of that coffin as it was raised. I remember, too, the rueful smile and comment of Home Office analyst Dr. Roche Lynch as he saw the water spill out: 'Not a chance!' he said to his assistants.

At the inquest which followed, the coroner was told by witnesses that in her fifteen years of married life Mrs. Rosse had never once expressed any wish to be buried anywhere near the River Thames. Sir Bernard Spilsbury told him he could find no trace whatever of cerebral haemorrhage or of Bright's Disease. Dr. Roche Lynch said he found no trace of poison.

He also said, however, that the top of the unsealed coffin was only eight inches below ground level—the shallowest grave he had ever seen. He added that the body must have been immersed in water for months as the churchyard was constantly flooded. About that flooding he said: 'In view of the time that has elapsed since death, and the condition to which the body has been subjected, it is quite possible that certain poisons could have been decomposed, thus rendering their detection impossible.'

There could be no doubt in anyone's mind where the finger of suspicion was pointing.

The coroner said this: 'Mr. Maundy Gregory appears to have been a man of some substance. But towards the beginning of 1932 his financial position became rapidly worse, until, about August, he was in difficulties owing some thousands of pounds and apparently not having funds wherewith to discharge his debts.

'I do not wish to emphasise the point which has been mentioned that certain drugs do decompose when exposed, or when they have been buried in soil, waterlogged or otherwise. All I will say is that no poison has been found, and therefore no possible charge can arise out of this inquiry, and there must be . . . an open verdict.'

Maundy Gregory himself was not present to hear those words. He was just out of prison. Now he had defied a subpoena to attend the inquest and fled the country. My office told me to find him. Within a few days I traced him to Paris and went across to interview him once more.

I found him living in style—on Mrs. Rosse's £18,000. He was as glib as ever. He knew from the coroner's words he was clear of any possible poisoning charge. He told me his life with Mrs. Rosse was 'no vulgar intrigue' but a brother and sister relationship.

He told me about the mystery illness which ended in her death. 'I was having lunch with [ex] King George of Greece,' he said, 'in the West End of London when a telephone call came from the house in St. John's Wood urging me to come home at once. Naturally I did so. When I reached the house I went to her bedside.

' "Quick!" she cried. "Pen and paper!" '

Gregory told me how he fumbled through his pockets and found only one thing to write on: the menu card from the restaurant he had just left. The will was written there and then. She lived till next day, he said. At the moment she died he was having yet another lunch with the former King of Greece. Why? 'I felt . . . no good purpose would be served by postponing it.' And, he told me, after he knew she was dead he went in search of a burial place 'by the riverside, where many of our happiest hours had been spent'.

He had great trouble in finding such a graveyard. In the end—so anxious was he for a grave by the water—he offered one hundred guineas to the Parish fund if permission could be given. To get it, Maundy Gregory, faithful friend, needed the consent of a warden of the church. He found such a warden—a butler—playing cards at a village whist drive, hauled him out and persuaded him to sign the necessary papers.

I

Why did he do it? Why was the grave ordered to be so shallow? 'I did not like to think there should be a great weight of earth over poor Mrs. Rosse, so I ordered . . . as shallow a grave as possible should be dug, and also gave instructions that the cofin should not be sealed.'

Maundy Gregory never came back to London. I have always believed that when the £18,000 from Mrs. Rosse ran out he lived on cash gratefully provided by those newly-titled gentlemen who had evaded all talk of scandal by his plea of Guilty at Bow Street.

I never had any proof. I relate the facts now as an unfinished story. Gregory is long dead, and we do not know for sure how he died. He was still in Paris when the city was overrun by Hitler's troops in 1940. The German authorities were a sight tougher with him than our own had been. The Gestapo took him, and he was reported dead within a year of imprisonment by that black band. Maybe, before he died, he paid some of his debt to the Britain he had cheated for so many years. It is in his favour that some believe he might have died because he refused to broadcast, as another Haw-Haw, for the Nazis.

After the war I went back to Paris to try to find out what had happened to Maundy Gregory. I browsed through the official records. His death was recorded, but not the cause.

Mister Fixit's death was as efficiently hushed up as he himself had silenced the threatened 'Honours Scandal' of yester-year.

This man fascinated me as few others have done. I always rated him king of the confidence tricksters. I am quite sure in my own mind he got away with murder. Just as I believe he made a fat living after his imprisonment from blackmail, and tried to use my name—Percy Hoskins, *Daily Express* crime reporter—as part of the blackmail plot.

When he first fled to Paris, he had Mrs. Rosse's money to live on. But he was a spender: in his business, the confidence trickster business, you have to speculate to accumulate later, and whenever funds began to get low, he would telephone

London. A little while later, across the Channel and by train
to Paris would travel one Peter Mazzina, once head waiter
at the famous London club where Gregory entertained the
snobs who wanted to buy a title. Mazzina, who later committed suicide, was a confidant of Gregory's and the perfect
instrument for blackmail since he had personally witnessed
each meeting.

Mazzina came to me after Gregory had first left for Paris
and wanted to know if the *Daily Express* was interested in
buying Gregory's memoirs. Assuming one could believe the
man, such memoirs were potential dynamite. Not only would
Gregory name the men who bought their titles, he would
also have to disclose who it was in high office who had taken
bribes and made the necessary arrangements.

But here was the rub. We had only Gregory's word to go
on. It was in his power to blacken anyone, and it would be
enormously difficult, maybe impossible, to find substantive
evidence. He was certain to ask a small fortune for information
which, because of the laws of libel, could well prove unusable.

I promised to write to Gregory and let him know, after
consulting my Editor, Arthur Christiansen. Some sixth sense
stopped me from sending any letter. As in all dealings with
Maundy Gregory, there was never any proof, but gradually I
came to realise that all he wanted was a letter signed Percy
Hoskins, on *Daily Express* headed notepaper, irrespective of
what it contained.

He would then go to all the rich fools who had paid him to
secure them a title and say 'The *Daily Express* is buying my
memoirs. See, here's a letter from their crime man, Hoskins'—
a quick glimpse of letter and signature to follow—'and what
will it be worth to keep your name out of the scandal to
follow?'

Mazzina kept after me but although I saw Gregory personally in Paris, I never wrote. I never had the slightest doubt
that he blackmailed all his 'clients' by threatening to expose
them in his memoirs, but at least he had no help from me.

# 16  The Poisoner

Poison lends itself most conveniently to the dream of perfect murder. Use a gun, and the commotion will bring every copper for miles around, and the tell-tale mark of the firing pin is as damning as any fingerprint.

Strangle, and the pathologist will find you out, even if you fake murder to look like suicide by hanging *and* bury the body afterwards.

Chop the victim into pieces, dismember, drop the segments in tightly wrapped parcels into the sea and still the Murder Squad will triumph: witness the human wild animal called Hume caged in his Swiss prison.

Do what you will to escape detection: burn the body; suffocate; rain blows on the skull from behind; electrocute; knife; destroy the whole human frame, bones and all, in a tank full of acid; hide the corpse so well no man will ever set eyes on it again; push it through a ship's porthole and feed it to the sharks (as James Camb did to 'Gay' Gibson) and even then stand trial for murder.

But poison: there you have a chance to get off scot-free. It is so easy to administer. The victim is hungry or thirsty and, in any case, unsuspecting.

And, if you do your homework sufficiently well, you may hit upon a poison that leaves no trace at all. I know of one, not too difficult to obtain, where the apparent effect is one of heart failure . . . with no trace of poison left in the system. That is the great attraction of poison to the murderer: the protection afforded by its worm-like stealth.

There are others. It is a weapon well suited to the weak, hence its popularity with women. And it is a joy to possess and use if you hate someone enough: of all methods of murder, here is the most painful, sly, and cruel. Poisons like arsenic, the commonest and easiest to obtain, guarantee a monstrously agonising end.

For all these reasons, poison has been a popular method of killing since the time of the Borgias. What is rare is to find motiveless poisoning. It seems inconceivable that any man should plan murder this way merely to see if it can pass undetected—or does it?

Of all the cases that have come my way in this specialised field of poison, the Barlow case rates a mention on two counts. He committed the first known case of murder through injection of insulin—his wife was a non-diabetic, so it led to her collapse and drowning in the bath—and he did it for no reason anyone can discover. The only conclusion I can draw from the known facts is that he believed he could get away with murder by insulin and experimented accordingly.

Kenneth Barlow, aged thirty-eight, lived with his wife Elizabeth in a terraced two-up and two-down in Thornbury Crescent, Bradford, in Yorkshire. He was a male nurse and worked in St. Luke's Hospital in the West Riding town of Huddersfield. She had a local job, in a laundry. They had been married less than a year. They seemed to be ideally happy. The neighbours found them a happy and apparently easy-going pair.

On the night of 3 May, 1957, between 11 p.m. and midnight, Kenneth Barlow hammered on his neighbour's door and shouted to them to call the doctor—*quickly*. He said his wife had passed out in the bath, and he had found her with her head under water; he had tried artificial respiration without success. Then he ran back indoors, to continue artificial respiration, until the doctor arrived.

Barlow had his story off pat when first the doctor and then an observant Detective Sergeant called Naylor from Bradford CID called round. His wife was tired that night, said Barlow, and had gone to bed early. He put the child (from his previous marriage) to bed himself, went round and locked up in the normal way, and went upstairs some time later.

About 10 p.m. Mrs. Barlow, who had complained of the heat, said she now felt better and was going to take a bath. Right, said Kenneth Barlow, and promptly dozed off: came to about 11 p.m., found his wife had not come back to bed, then noticed the light still on in the bathroom. He went in to find her unconscious, with her head well under water. He pulled the plug out at once and began to administer first aid. Now he stood in the hallway, cool and composed although naturally sad, to greet doctor and detective as they arrived.

*Both of them* noticed how the pupils of her eyes were dilated, as though she were under the influence of some drug. Sergeant Naylor also spotted one curious thing: Barlow's pyjamas were bone dry, although—on his own admission—he was wearing them when he tried to revive poor Elizabeth Barlow. The alarm bells that ring to warn every good policeman things are not as straightforward as they seem sounded that night in the house in Thornbury Crescent, and Naylor called his superiors right away.

The Chief Constable of Bradford, Mr. H. S. Price, went to the house. He looked at the body. He too was baffled by those dry pyjamas and another factor: lack of water on the walls and floor. Curious, when the bath was full enough to drown Mrs. Barlow, that the attempts to lift her out and give artificial respiration had not even left one puddle on the bathroom floor.

He called in Dr. David Price, the West Riding pathologist and the senior inspector from the Harrogate laboratories. Dilation of the pupils seemed a sure indication that Mrs. Barlow was drugged when she died. The police found syringes in the house, but Barlow was a male nurse and his story that he had used one to give himself penicillin for a carbuncle on the neck seemed reasonable.

The body was taken to the mortuary for post mortem and extensive tests for poisons and drugs. More scientists were called in next day but immediate tests again showed nothing traceable in the system. What Dr. Price did find, however, were four tiny red dots in the buttocks similar to marks left by hypodermic injection. He cut away the flesh around and below both sets of punctures and ascertained that they had been made shortly before her collapse and death in the bath.

More specialists were called in for consultation: Professor C. S. Russell, a gynaecologist from Sheffield (Mrs. Barlow was found to be in the early stages of pregnancy); Professor Thompson, from Guy's Hospital in London; and a senior chemist from Boots' factory at Nottingham. They had to weigh the symptoms shown by Mrs. Barlow before death— including her collapse before sliding under the level of the bathwater.

Insulin, of course, is not a poison in the sense that arsenic is. It is extensively used in the treatment of diabetics to reduce the sugar content of the blood. If it is injected into a non-diabetic, that person goes into a state of shock and collapse. So, if the bath should be full enough, such a fainting fit could well prove fatal.

Insulin? There was no known case of injection by insulin in the course of murder. Here was a completely virgin field of research for the combined Murder Squad—police backed by the scientists. While Dr. Price and his colleagues concentrated on laboratory experiments, the police stepped up their inquiries into Barlow's background.

In the laboratory, samples taken from the flesh cut away from Mrs. Barlow's body were injected into mice. Other mice were injected with insulin. The results were identical. The creatures went into a state of collapse and died. Guinea pigs were used in the same way with the same result. The human tissues were then injected with anti-insulin compounds and used again on the mice and guinea pigs, but this time, with the insulin destroyed deliberately, there were no ill effects. So it *was* insulin that was used to murder Mrs. Barlow.

In the CID headquarters at Bradford every precaution was taken not to forewarn Barlow of their line of inquiry. Discreet checks were made at the hospital where he worked to see what medicines and drugs he had access to, and how much —if any—was unaccounted for. There was professional evidence aplenty that he often gave injections of insulin to patients.

Barlow was charged with the murder of his wife. All through the period of arrest and trial he protested his innocence.

Sir Harry Hylton-Foster, then Solicitor-General, led the prosecution. It is not the easiest of cases to take through the court, in spite of the magnificent backroom work by Dr. Price and his associates.

Here you had a man and wife, known to be happy together, married less than a year. No shred of evidence as to any quarrel or bad feeling between them, no sudden blazing row that could have ended in a resolve to murder. What could the motive have been? There was no suggestion of gain. There was no hint of jealousy, no rumour of another man or woman in the marital background.

Barlow's story of how those two syringes came to be found in his house was still convincing enough. Traces of penicillin *had* been found on the one he said he used for the boil on his neck, and he said both he and his wife had used the other. She had given her father injections of morphia, he said, to ease the pain of cancer; and he had used it on her for injections of a drug called ergometrine, to end her pregnancy—at her own request.

He also said she had had fainting fits before: once in the bath, and he described how he had rescued her just in time on that occasion.

Sir Harry called on three witnesses who had heard Barlow

refer to insulin in the past as one means to the 'perfect murder'. There was male nurse Harry Stork, who had worked with Barlow in a sanatorium in the middle 'fifties. He recalled Barlow saying it would be difficult to detect afterwards as it dissolved in the bloodstream.

A former patient at the same sanatorium remembered a conversation with Barlow who said of insulin: 'Get a load of this, and it's the quickest way out.' Then there was a woman nurse who had tended diabetics with Barlow, and remembered him saying: 'You could kill somebody with insulin as it can't be found very easily—unless you use a very large dose.'

There was, however, a significant weakness implicit in this line of prosecution argument. Barlow had been married to Elizabeth less than one year. Was the jury to believe he was already contemplating the murder of a wife he had yet to meet?

The defence, led by Mr. Bernard Gillies QC, called as their expert witness Dr. Hobson, from St. Luke's Hospital in London. He told the court that in moments of stress (like anger, for instance, *or fear*) the human body automatically releases and pumps adrenalin into the bloodstream. This in turn raises the sugar level—which could produce an increase of insulin as a natural reaction.

'If [Mrs. Barlow] knew she was slipping down and drowning in the bath,' he said, 'and that she could not get out, she would be terrified and I think that would produce all the symptoms the chemists have described.'

Against this was the amount of insulin found below those hypodermic syringe marks in the woman's body. Insulin produced naturally in the way Dr. Hobson described would be evenly distributed over the body—and it would need a fantastic amount to reach the overall level found round those puncture marks.

The judge told the jury: 'If you are satisfied he injected insulin into his wife and knowingly injected it, you will probably find no difficulty in reaching the decision that he did so with intent to kill.'

Mr. Justice Diplock told them to make up their minds, saying 'This is murder or nothing'. The jury found for murder. Barlow was sentenced to life imprisonment, and a new page had been written in British criminal history.

Apart from my constant checks through Scotland Yard, I took no part in the police investigation before Barlow was finally charged. This was a matter for my associates in the northern offices of the *Daily Express*. What fascinated me, and took me to the trial, was the knowledge that this was to be the first trial for murder by insulin injection in any murder investigation.

I have discussed the case many times since with many an expert and always our talks have ended with the one question: why did he do it?

Barlow's first wife had died in 1956 at the early age of thirty-three. Even after the inquest, doubt existed over the precise cause of her death, although it was found to be from natural causes. If his protestations of innocence at the time of his trial for the murder of Elizabeth, his second wife, were genuine, then here was someone who had been dealt a doubly cruel blow by Fate.

But if the verdict was just—that he committed 'a cold, cruel and carefully premeditated murder' as the judge said—even though he was happily married, we are left with only one possible conclusion. Here was a man who really believed he had found the way to commit the 'perfect murder' and so carried it out as a cold-blooded and clinical experiment. On his new wife, who unfortunately happened to be the most convenient human guinea pig.

If his method of murder was unique, it shows Barlow held at least one trait in common with all poisoners: a callous disregard for suffering. He would have done well in any Nazi wartime concentration camp.

# 17　A King Stumbles on Murder

It is a scene which has always gripped my imagination: a
King coming home unannounced, and tapping his foot with
annoyance to find the milk still outside his front door at three
in the afternoon. . . .

*Date*: 9 June, 1946.

*Place*: 45 Chester Square, in London's Belgravia, residence
in exile for ex-King George of Greece whose own country
had been overrun by Hitler and then plunged into civil war.

*Situation*: King George's housekeeper is lying murdered in
her rooms, shot through the back of the head at close range as
she tried to get to the telephone. Without knowing it—she lay
behind locked doors, and not all the King's men could find
the key—His Majesty had stumbled on a murder that was to
set a blaze of excitement running through the émigré world of
those post-war days.

To use the royal parlance of more recent years, Scotland
Yard really 'pulled its finger out' over this one. It's not every
day that dead bodies are found in the house of a king. Two
of the finest Murder Squad men of the day, Deputy Commander Bill Rawlings and Detective Superintendent John Ball,
were assigned to the investigation.

It was not a particularly complicated case: steady digging
into the love life of the murdered housekeeper, Miss Elizabeth
McLindon, soon produced the suspect who was later to be
tried and hanged. But one thing that emerged—yet again in

a murder case—was the ease with which intelligent women fall for men with the murkiest of pasts, the simplicity with which they are fooled by the clumsiest of forgeries.

They say love is blind. Even so, you would expect a woman steady and capable enough of rising to the post of King's housekeeper to be shrewder than most in her judgment of people. Miss McLindon woke up to the duplicity of her lover too late to save her own life.

Fuming with annoyance at finding a 'deserted' household, the King left on 9 June. Nearly a week passed before his housekeeper's body was discovered. The police broke into her rooms on 14 June when it was clear something untoward had happened with the tradesmen turned away, the telephone calls unanswered, the milk bottles steadily accumulating on the royal doorstep.

There was no sign of a struggle. Forty-one-year-old Elizabeth McLindon had been shot from behind as she sat in a chair, with the telephone by her side. A .32 cartridge case lay on the carpet where it had been ejected. There had been no break-in. Nothing was stolen. It looked as though she had been trying to make a telephone call at the moment she was shot. Rawlings and Ball began to look for human frailties—like an ill-starred love affair—that might explain such a murder.

Every lead had to come from the dead woman. Apart from the .32 cartridge case (no gun was found) there was nothing else to work on. First man to their aid was the police surgeon. He estimated death occurred on 8 June, the day before the King's call. The Murder Squad detectives knocked on every door asking for memories to be racked to recall anything out of the ordinary in sedate Chester Square on 8 June.

You have read that phrase, or something like it, in the newspaper accounts of a thousand crimes. It sounds so *dull*, so *routine*. So it is: but it is hard work, vitally important work, and in the days of the hangman, often with a man's life depending on the shrewdness and patience of the questioners.

I have lost count of the times I have driven to the scene of a murder and watched the teams at work: big men, in trilby hats, direct but courteous, ringing and knocking at countless hundreds of white doors, blue doors, oak doors and cedar doors, yellow doors and brown doors; doors without a knocker or bell so you bend down and call through the letter-box; doors that open wide and offer a cup of tea, doors that open a fraction on a chain; doors that reveal friendly faces, doors that open on fear and hatred of the law; doors that have nothing to hide, doors that close on too many untold secrets.

It was harder work than usual, that day in Chester Square. It is a fairly snooty, that is to say reserved, square, and neighbours simply do not pry on neighbours or even *look* very often at what is going on outside. It was just after the war and men and women who had been forced to spend years in barrack rooms and huts with scores of other men and women now had a natural yearning for privacy and insularity: they didn't *want* to know what their neighbours were doing.

The Murder Squad reminded them: 8 June, you remember, the day of the flypast of the Victory Air Pageant? With the Lancasters and Hurricanes and Spitfires roaring overhead to commemorate the first anniversary of peace in Europe? That had brought one or two into the street, sure enough. One who remembered Miss McLindon running like a hare out of the King's house and down the street, after slamming the door behind her. Others who remembered seeing a man hammering on the door soon afterward, then running off in the same direction as the housekeeper.

The royal household was searched top to bottom. The incoming mail was interesting. There was a letter from 'Arthur' written and posted on 7 June begging Elizabeth to let him know why she would not answer his telephone calls. It was postmarked Brighton.

From her employers before King George, whose service she had newly joined, Superintendent Ball traced her relatives. Miss McLindon's sister identified 'Arthur' as one Arthur

Robert Boyce, now in lodgings in Brighton. Ball and his sergeant left Victoria on the Brighton Belle to interview him.

Arthur Boyce looked a gentle sort of man. He was tall and thin and sad-faced, and wore spectacles. He was dreadfully upset to learn that the woman he hoped to marry had been murdered. He told the policemen of other men she knew and volunteered the possibility that someone who hated the émigré King might have called at that house in Chester Square—perhaps with assassination in mind—only to kill Elizabeth, the housekeeper, instead.

Ball checked with Records and discovered that Arthur Robert Boyce had served eighteen months in jail for bigamy. He was wanted for questioning over the cashing of certain cheques, one of which had been altered after signature by Mr. Papanikolaou, secretary to King George of Greece. Not such a gentle man, after all!

Down on Brighton Pier, where Boyce worked as a painter, the Yard men spoke to his mates. One of them remembered him showing off a pistol—not so uncommon in those immediate post-war days—and saying it was loaded with 'five up the spout'. Boyce told him later he had thrown it into the sea. If this was the murder weapon and Boyce had really thrown it somewhere in the sea off Brighton Pier or the beach, the police were going to have a hard time linking it with the spent cartridge case found on the floor in Chester Square.

Superintendent Ball, blessed like so many of his Murder Squad colleagues with a rare gift of patience, went back to Boyce's lodgings and searched them. He examined every piece of paper he came across with particular care; he tagged anything he thought remotely interesting and filed it away; then he took Boyce to London for further questioning.

Among the fragments of paper this human squirrel collected in that flat was a luggage label, addressed to a Mr. John Rowland of Caernarvon in Wales. Ball booked Arthur Boyce on a fraud charge (a holding charge) and looked for Rowland: why, he wasn't altogether sure, but in the main to talk about

Boyce. Rowland was in the Army. Superintendent Ball found him—and got the break his patience had earned.

Rowland had once shared rooms with Boyce, and he had owned a .32 automatic pistol which had disappeared. He always believed Boyce had stolen it and had once written demanding its return, but his letter had never been answered.

'All right,' said the Yard man, masking his disappointment at being so near and yet so far from clinching his case. 'What about ammunition? Do you have a cartridge case fired from the pistol?'

Rowland said he thought there might be one in his house. He had fired the gun to test it, and kept one cartridge case as a base for adhesive tape. If it hadn't been thrown away—yes, that would be in his house still. Forensic tests showed that this cartridge case had been fired from the same gun that killed Elizabeth McLindon.

Boyce had murdered her because she found him out. When he proposed, Boyce had altered his bank account to read £2,075 in credit—the real figure was £75. All went well until he tried to buy the engagement ring.

He sat in the King's house in Chester Square and went through a selection that a West End jeweller gladly brought round to such an address. He picked one that cost £175 and lost his nerve as he wrote out the cheque, faltering over the simple spelling of the word 'hundred'. The jeweller held on to his rings until the cheque was presented. It bounced. Boyce initialled the alteration and it bounced again. Poor Miss McLindon learned all this from the jeweller on the day she died.

She already harboured growing suspicions about her 'fiancé'. She found an invitation to a wedding between Boyce and another woman in his coat and she wanted to know what it meant. She wrote to the woman for an explanation—and found this was the 'wedding' for which he had been imprisoned for bigamy. So she had hung up on Boyce whenever he telephoned.

She had run out of the house on 8 June, Victory Air Pageant day, when she learned he was on his way round. He had followed her, persuaded her to go back into the King's house with him—and then shot her as she reached for the telephone to ring the jeweller and confront him with one more lie.

My old friend Derek Curtis-Bennett, Q.C.—the eminent defence lawyer—did his best for Boyce at the trial for murder which followed. Boyce stuck to his theory that men who hated the King in exile were continually calling at the house in that Belgravia square, and that he had given Elizabeth the gun for protection.

Curtis-Bennett let the jury ponder that one. And also advanced a more ingenious theory. Had she been killed by a jealous lover rather than a political enemy of the King?

He said: 'Boyce was one of her lovers. How many others she had we do not know. One thing is certain, Boyce was the reigning lover.

'Suppose this woman of many loves had yet another one? What better way of getting rid of Boyce on the afternoon of 8 June than to say the King was going to the house that night: telling Boyce to sleep at Brighton and then letting in, not the King of Greece, but the king of her heart at the time?'

The jury had no doubts. They returned a verdict of guilty and Arthur Boyce, that sad-faced, gaunt and unlikely-looking Romeo, was later hanged.

The story of the King who, all unknowing, stumbled on murder has been told many times in many countries. I tell it again now because to my mind the investigation that followed shows all that is best in the Murder Squad make-up at Scotland Yard. Tenacity, imagination, patience, teamwork—regal qualities for a royal murder hunt.

# 18   Strip Jack Naked

In the space of a year, between the winters of 1964 and 1965, six prostitutes were found murdered within a few miles of the centre of London. All six were stripped naked. All had been assaulted by a sexual pervert.

The killer was never found. The murders came to an end after the suicide of the Number One suspect. But while he was at large, the street-walkers of London lived through a reign of terror unequalled since the days of Jack the Ripper, eighty years earlier.

The murders were discovered with trip-hammer regularity. They became the talk not just of London but of England and the whole of the western world. The public here at home became seriously alarmed, and Scotland Yard was put under enormous pressure to find the Beast of the Thames. Men were taken from every division—CID and uniformed—and very brave policewomen volunteered to pose as prostitutes and parade themselves in the dangerous night streets. Their protection during these hazardous patrols came from detectives who lurked in the background and posed as ponces, those human leeches who live off the earnings of their tarts.

Many of my friends in the CID took part in the gigantic murder hunt. As the numbers of victims mounted, so the teams were co-ordinated under the leadership of one of the Yard's finest detectives, Assistant Commissioner John du Rose. He was a Det. Chief Superintendent at the time and had just begun a holiday when he was recalled to lead the hunt.

K

*Nude victim number 1* was thirty-year-old Hannah Tailford, of Thurlby Road, West Norwood, in the London suburbs. Dark-haired Hannah was found wedged under a floating pier in the River Thames near Hammersmith Bridge on 2 February, 1964.

She was naked apart from her stockings, which trailed in the black water round her ankles. The sex-maniac who killed her had gagged her, possibly believing she was not quite dead, by ramming her briefs in her mouth. There was no sign of her clothing, which included a winter overcoat. Her handbag was also missing. Inside was the diary she kept listing the names and 'phone numbers of her many men friends.

Hannah was an old hand at the world's oldest game, and she had four convictions for prostitution. At the time of her death she was using (as do so many of London's whores) a number of aliases, Hannah or Anne Lynch—she lived once with a man named Lynch and had a child by him—Anne Taylor and Teresa Bell.

She came from Heddon-on-the-Wall in Northumberland and plied her trade in the West End, Pimlico and Belgravia. Her 'speciality', and the one which led to her death, was the car pick-up and tantalising strip in the back seat.

Hannah had one special friend, a foreign diplomat serving in London. He called on her from time to time to perform at wild kinky parties, sex orgies in the 'upper crust' houses of Kensington. Scotland Yard immediately got in touch with the Foreign Office to pursue inquiries. The diplomat concerned had left Britain soon after Hannah's body was discovered, but later returned. He was later ruled out as a suspect.

There was a strong possibility that Hannah had been murdered, because of the stripping of the body and the gag in the mouth, for example: *but no proof.* Suicides do take their clothes off before taking their own lives, and the Thames gives up two dead bodies a week on average.

Result: doubts in everyone's mind, but an 'open verdict' returned at the inquest.

*Nude victim number 2* was Irene Lockwood, aged twenty-six, and just five feet in height. She was found on 8 April, two months after the first victim, at Dukes Meadows in Chiswick: body number two in the Thames!

Irene was completely nude. Her clothing was obviously missing, as with Hannah Tailford, to delay identification. Lockwood was tattooed—a great many prostitutes are. On her arm it said 'John, in memory.'

She was well known in the West End—where she was available to star in blue movies—and the sleazier areas of King's Cross and Islington. She dabbled in every kind of sex kinks, and like Hannah Tailford she specialised in the car kerb trade. She knew the risks involved. A year earlier her best friend Vicki Pender (alias Walsh) had been found murdered after a session of 'reefers' with an ex-soldier, who was later convicted and jailed for life.

The Lockwood case came under Det. Superintendent Frank Davies, who was later to win promotion as Head of the Flying Squad. Before his inquiries had given any real lead, a man came forward and 'confessed' to killing Lockwood and throwing her body into the Thames. He was a crank. He spent two months in jail before he was officially found 'not guilty' and set free. Meantime there were other developments to harass the police.

*Nude victim number 3,* Helen Barthelemy, only twenty-two, was found on 24 April, just sixteen days after the discovery of Irene Lockwood's body.

Helen was found, by a young man on his way to work, in a lane at Brentford—less than one mile from the Thames. Like the first two victims, she was naked. Marks on the body showed her briefs had been removed by the killer after death. Some of her teeth were missing—one broken fragment of tooth was lodged in her throat. There was nothing to show she had been hit by a fist, or beaten up before death. She was tattooed.

Poor Helen Barthelemy had packed a lot of incident into her twenty-two years. She had worked in a circus, flying through the air on a trapeze; graduated to stripper on Blackpool's 'Golden Mile'; and already, in 1963, had been sentenced to four years in prison for luring a man client on to the sands where he was beaten and robbed. She would probably have been alive today if she had served her time. But, alas for Helen, her conviction was set aside on appeal and back she came to the bright lights—and murder.

Her life in London set the police on to false trails for some time. She liked coloured men. She lived with coloured families in Notting Hill in London. The last man to see her alive was a West Indian who, with his family, lived in that same house. Helen was a pot smoker, she had drug addicts among her customers, and she was attracted to vice like a moth to a candle. With hindsight you can say—as I do—she was a 'cinch' for the Thames-side prowler.

The Yard now had a considerable force concentrating on the nude murders. The Tailford inquiries were headed by Detective Inspector Frank Ridge, head of Thames Police CID. Superintendent Davies led the Lockwood investigation. Superintendent Maurice Osborne, another superb detective and specialist in murder, directed inquiries into the Barthelemy killing. Each had a big squad working under him and they were driven hard in a race to catch the murderer before he struck again.

Scotland Yard's fears that the sex-crazy Thameside killer would strike again are clearly shown in their appeal dated 28 April, 1964. It was directed to the six thousand prostitutes who offer 'love' for sale on the streets of London. *Six thousand!*

It said: 'During the past five months the bodies of four naked women have been found either in or near the River Thames between Hammersmith and Chiswick.

'The women concerned are: Gwyneth Rees, alias Tina Smart [later ruled out as a victim of this murderer] found buried in a refuse dump near Chiswick Bridge on 8 November, 1963;

'Hannah Tailford, found drowned near Hammersmith Bridge on 2 February, 1964;

'Irene Lockwood, alias Sandra Russell, found drowned at Dukes Meadows near Barnes Bridge in April 1964;

'Helen Catherine Barthelemy, alias Helen Paul, found strangled in an alleyway at Brentford on 8 April, 1964.

'All the dead women were prostitutes, and all were frequenters of low class cafés and clubs. It is known in two of the cases at least, they favoured coloured men. In no case has their clothing been found.

'They usually picked up clients from streets or clubs in the central and West London areas, and often went with them in motor vehicles.

'Inquiries on these lines by the Murder teams have brought to light cases where women have been persuaded to enter cars, and there forced to strip under threats of violence, and in one case under the threat of a knife.

'In some cases violence has actually been used and the women concerned are fortunate not to have been killed.

*'Police fear that if information is not forthcoming, yet another prostitute may be found dead.*

'Although there is no evidence as yet to indicate that all the deaths were caused by one man, it is a possibility. The four murder teams are now co-ordinating their inquiries and all are operating from Shepherd's Bush police station.

'In particular police wish to interview any prostitute who has been made to strip and assaulted. The identity of any woman wishing to give information to police will not be divulged, and if she will communicate either by letter or telephone to Scotland Yard (WHI 1212) or Shepherd's Bush police station (Shepherd's Bush 1113) stating she wishes to give information, a member of the Special Squad of male and female officers will meet her where and when she wishes.

'This appeal is urgently directed to all those women whose means of livelihood place them in danger of meeting the same fate.'

This huge and unprecedented publicity had its effect. For a variety of possible reasons—fear on the part of the murderer, or caution among the London prostitutes—no more bodies were found for three months.

*Nude victim number 4* was found on 14 July. She was Mary Fleming, aged thirty-one, found in a cul-de-sac in Berrymead Road, Acton, two miles from the spot where Helen Barthelemy had been dumped. She was totally naked, and her clothes were missing. She was known to haunt low-class cafés and clubs.

Mary Fleming, alias Mary Turner, was the mother of two children and living apart from her husband. One of her 'specialities' was to offer love for sale in the back of a car. She had been strangled or asphyxiated.

She was last seen alive in Queensway, London, some days before her body was found. That was at five o'clock on this bright summer's morning of 14 July by Mr. George Heard, a chauffeur who lived opposite the point where she was dumped. A car was heard to stop there, start up and drive away before the body was actually found.

On 2 November, 1964, the adjourned inquests on Barthelemy and Fleming were resumed. Verdict: murder by person or persons unknown. The Yard's urgent warning had been ignored and its fears realised.

One vital clue had come from the police laboratories after examination of their two bodies, and it was kept secret by the Murder Squads. In both cases, dirt found on the naked bodies was discovered to contain traces of paint used on cars. It was so fine that it could only have come from a high-pressure paint spray gun. From a paint spray shop? A garage? A do-it-yourself kit? There were endless possibilities. Another huge search was begun by the weary Murder Squads working out of Shepherd's Bush police station.

They were still toiling away when the news broke that *Nude victim number 5* had been found. She was Margaret McGowan, alias Frances Brown, aged twenty-two, a prostitute who had made her way south from her native Glasgow. She was found on a rubbish tip in a car park in Kensington, completely naked, with all her clothes missing; tattooed; strangled or asphyxiated; one tooth missing when found.

Under the alias Frances Brown, she had given evidence at the famous trial of Dr. Stephen Ward, at the Old Bailey in 1963, where there was so much talk of orgies and whipping and perversions. This fact brought another burden on to the Murder teams. Every witness in the Stephen Ward case had to be traced and interviewed to see if they could help.

Like the others, Margaret McGowan ignored the warnings and climbed into one car back seat too many. She was drinking heavily with another prostitute on the night of 23 October, 1964, when they were both picked up by men in separate cars. She was never seen alive again. The second prostitute went to the police at Shepherd's Bush and from her information Identikit pictures of both men were built up and published in every newspaper. It was no use: the two were afraid to come forward.

Demand for 'copy' from our papers was insatiable. Like the police, we crime reporters were working round the clock. Here was a world story, the most terrifying crime story since the days of the 'Ripper'.

All through the early winter months, the search went on, to the point of near exhaustion. The search for the unknown killer, the questioning of innumerable suspects, the search for a vehicle vaguely believed to be either a small van or shooting brake, and the search for the all-important spray shop.

Then, a year after the discovery of Hannah Tailford's body in the Thames, *Nude victim number 6* turned up in a West London alleyway. She was Bridie O'Hara, born in Dublin, and another prostitute. Like the others, she was small (5ft. 2in.), completely naked when found, she was tattooed, and some of her teeth were missing. She had been asphyxiated. There was no sign of her clothing.

Bridie was last seen alive on the night of 11 January, 1965, as she left a Shepherd's Bush pub at closing time. She died soon afterwards. Her body was not found until 16 February, but it was in such a good state of preservation it was clear she had been stored somewhere under cover until the coast was clear for dumping. Her body was closely examined, and once more the laboratories found traces of the same car paint-spray and dust.

Its discovery resulted in a tremendous hue and cry. This new inquiry came under Detective Superintendent William Baldock, for the body was found in his Division.

At this point Chief Superintendent John du Rose abandoned his holiday after a call from the Yard, and returned to London to take overall charge of the whole investigation.

The paint-spray shop was traced, to a factory estate in Acton. Any car could drive through the site easily enough— but the killer was certainly among the drivers, so each car that crossed the checkpoint now had to be traced and closely examined.

It was a tall order. No owner, no matter who it might be, escaped the police examination. One of my colleagues on the *Daily Express* came into this category. That in itself was mildly embarrassing: then the police found traces of blood in the boot! It came from a hare he had shot, but there were considerable alarums and excursions before that essential fact was established.

Du Rose's complete Murder Squad, reinforced by the Special Patrol Group and men and women from the uniformed branch, now numbered six hundred in all. There has never been a bigger one in the history of Scotland Yard. They gave du Rose everything they had to give, in spirit and cheerfulness and devotion to duty—a duty that as far as the women police decoys were concerned was highly dangerous and unpleasant—while John du Rose, a man whose friendship I value, was an inspiration to them all.

It takes nothing from their reputation that they failed to arrest and charge the Thameside Terror. Du Rose was quite certain he knew his man and opened a war of nerves to try to break him down.

I quote here from his own book *Murder Was my Business* (W. H. Allen):

'In this war of nerves important clues were leaked in day-to-day bulletins covering our activities in many areas. The original number of suspects was given at twenty, but these were gradually scaled down until it was revealed that of the three that remained, one was known to be the killer.

'We could never forget the fact that no woman was safe until the killer was in our hands, but it was not to be; and within a month of the murder of Bridie O'Hara the man I wanted to arrest took his own life.

'Without a shadow of doubt the weight of our investigation and the inquiries we had made about him led to the killer committing suicide.

'We had done all we possibly could, but faced with his death no positive evidence was available to prove or disprove our belief that he was in fact the man we had been seeking.

'Because he was never arrested, or stood trial, he must be considered innocent and will therefore never be named.'

I know, of course, the man's identity. So do a handful of other crime reporters, and the secret is safe with us. None of us, certainly not policemen, is judge and jury with power to find any man guilty in such circumstances.

But the facts speak for du Rose, and themselves. The spate of Nude Murders ended with that unnamed man's death.

When you consider the man-hours, the risks, the miles covered in questioning, the huge expense, the seemingly endless bypaths that opened up as each fragment of a clue came to light and were pursued to the end—to avenge the murder of six prostitutes—there can be no finer tribute to the finest name in all police history: Scotland Yard.

# Index of Persons